Sermons to Intellectuals

William Sloane Coffin, Jr. Helmut Gollwitzer Will Herberg
Francis B. Sayre, Jr.   Joseph Sittler   R. Gregor Smith

Sermons to Intellectuals

FROM THREE CONTINENTS

B. Davie Napier   Daniel T. Niles   Schubert M. Ogden   James A. Pike
Helmut Thielicke   Paul Tillich   Reinold von Thadden-Trieglaff

Edited by
FRANKLIN H. LITTELL

THE MACMILLAN COMPANY, NEW YORK
COLLIER-MACMILLAN LTD., LONDON

Translations from the German are the editor's, with the exception of the sermon by Reinold von Thadden-Trieglaff—where he gladly acknowledges his indebtedness to Miss Gisela Kanzler of the *Kirchentag* office.

Publishers' permissions are noted at the points of reference.

First Printing

The Macmillan Company, New York
Collier-Macmillan Canada Limited, Galt, Ontario
Divisions of The Crowell-Collier Publishing Company

Printed in the United States of America

Library of Congress catalog card number: 63–10003

DESIGN BY RICHARD A. KASELER

Contents

Introduction

To publish a book of sermons is today a sobering process. The statement is frequently heard that the age of great preaching is past. A few years ago a distinguished bishop of the Church of South India published a book, after a period of some months in the States, in which he discussed "the silence of the American pulpit." Among people who read and write, the sermon is now regarded as a debased form of currency, seldom treated seriously by men of letters and the literary journals. Yet there was a time when the sermon was a major literary form, and there were generations when the Protestant clergy—instead of suffering in feebleness the indignity of constant attack from the political underworld—proclaimed a message which shaped the affairs of men and nations.

There are plain historical reasons why the preachers have been reduced to the status of eunuchs, in a society which still appreciates as entertainers those to whom it denies potency and authority. The chief reason is that the extraordinary popularity of religion in America, at the end of a century and a half of mass accessions on a scale never surpassed in two millennia of church history, has been achieved by eliminating the "offense" of the Gospel. The proclaiming of the baptism of repentance which precedes the baptism of the Spirit (Acts 19:1-7) has been widely replaced by short cuts to "cheap grace." [1] Preparatory training for membership, grown minimal even on the books, has largely been removed. Promiscuity of membership practices is carried over from the doorway to the center, so that the most elementary standards—theological, ethical, moral, or even financial—have disappeared from the larger churches of the American social establishment. The note of discontinuity has been lost: nothing is predicted, or even expected, of church goers beyond the responses normal and measurable among persons of the same social, economic, and racial status. More than that, the cause of the Baals (the gods of fertility, of production) is again so well financed and promoted that the preacher who persists in proclaiming the words which are like a consuming fire may very well find himself dropped in the name of peace into some obscure denominational well.

Popular preaching has deteriorated because it has lost its essential quality of bindingness. Great preaching is preaching for a verdict. Great preaching is involved (*engagé*): it has foresworn the hands-in-pocket stance of the casual

[1] See the discussion in Dietrich Bonhoeffer's *The Cost of Discipleship* (London: S.C.M. Press, 1948), pp. 37f, of the situation in German Protestantism before the church struggle. As at many other points, the parallels of pre-Hitler German Protestantism to contemporary American Protestantism are startling.

observer. Great preaching has moral earnestness—not to be confused with the half-abashed repetition of petty legalisms and minor moralisms. Whatever else they are, great sermons are not entertainment. "Is it nothing to thee, all ye that pass by?!" The true sermon is not an essay—either in form or in style of delivery. A good sermon speaks to the condition of those present. Its purpose is proclamation, proclamation of God's action in history. Its style is interpretation, making real to those who have ears to hear the significance of the divine initiative for their lives.

A real problem of the American pulpit is that communication requires something to be related and a people to be addressed. With the blending of the churches into the background, that people to be addressed may be a "latent church" which stands outside precisely because the institutional church does not take her mission seriously. Today, the message which burns and heals is as apt to appear occasionally in the pages of *The Saturday Review, The Evergreen Review,* or *The American Scholar,* as in the official church press.

In the American churches of the nineteenth century, and especially following the trauma induced by the Civil War, the objective content of the message became more and more identified with "the American way of life" or perhaps "the southern way of life." And the inner content became identified with what is comonly called "spirituality" (precisely what the German Christians called *"Geistigkeit,"* in supporting Hitler)—enthusiasm, without credal or sacramental discipline or integrity. And recently we are brought to those peculiar excesses of culture-religion which mark the professional anti-Communists, the superpatriots, the Protestant nativists. At first it sounds as though we might be pressed back to self-examination, to repentance, to turn again to the God whose purpose we have rebelled against. But on closer inspection we perceive that this popular word, for all of its emotional effluvium, is not the Word which convicts and converts at all. It is not the Good News that makes all things new, but the bad news that everything must stay just the way it is. Its word is not the Word of prophecy, the Word that this adversary too shall pass away, but rather the word of appeasement—to the world and its demands. The liberty of preaching, too little used, is openly challenged. The "crown rights of the King," too seldom announced, are denied: "Why don't the preachers stay out of politics?" The most ancient heresy of all is put forward by the revolt of the unshepherded: that God and the church are there to be used to shore up unbaptized positions of worldly power.

All of this is part of the price being paid for verbalization which has lost its integrity, which is at best merely concerned with "ideals," which has lost contact with the historical situation and with that community which carries history. Precisely for this reason, in selecting sermons which do proclaim, which do carry the note of prophecy, which do speak to a Christian people of their true ministry, preachers are included from areas outside our island paradise—from the younger church and from the churches scarred by the struggle with totalitarianism. For the younger churchmen, moving out of the period of overseas control, and the men of the resistance to nazism and communism, having seen the idols of the Victorian Age and the *Wilhelminischen Zeitalter* destroyed by fire, no longer live in the nineteenth century continuum of religious-cultural-social-economic-political values which still weighs down a waterlogged and immobilized American Protestantism.

In America, however, there are places where great preaching is heard too. Significantly, these centers are most frequently those seminary and university communities which have participated with their brethren overseas in the rediscovery of theology ("thinking Christianly") which has come out of the agony of the church in the twentieth century. It is here that there are men who have lived through, day by day, the testing of the churches in Middle Europe and in Asia, Africa, and the islands of the sea. In doing so, they too have rediscovered the Bible, the church, the laity, and the power of the Holy Spirit.

All of the preachers here presented have been associated with the Student Christian Movement in one or more of its phases. It was the German S.C.M. which contributed mightily to the "Confessing Church" in the struggle with nazism. It was the World's Student Christian Federation which opened the way for the many later works of the ecumenical movement. During this period of transition in the American churches, as new signs of life are springing up in lay academies and theological study groups at the local level, vital preaching can be found especially on the border line where church and university meet.

Let none assume, however, that the rediscovery of biblical theology has simply resulted in nests of esoterics who can barely talk to each other—and not at all to the reading layman. On the contrary, the newest theological movement takes the world seriously—as well as its redeemer. In the words attributed to Bonhoeffer, "Christ died for the world, not for the church!" The one overriding characteristic of these sermons is that they are relevant: they communicate. They communicate because they have something to say, because they have taken the world seriously in all of its grandeur and misery, because these preachers know that in the final analysis the only true and Christian Word is one that a man signs with his name and with his life.

FRANKLIN H. LITTELL

Chicago Theological Seminary

The Word

by William Sloane Coffin, Jr.*

Some 2,600 years ago King Zedekiah of Judah climbed the ramparts of besieged Jerusalem. After surveying the panorama of impending annihilation, he ordered Jeremiah brought forth from the dungeon cell where he had been confined and asked him, "Is there any word from the Lord?"

A few weeks ago I was having breakfast in one of the small diners in Idlewild Airport, when suddenly there appeared a forlorn and rather desperate-looking Cuban, waving a nearly empty quart bottle of beer. In loud but very broken English he began to exhort the waiting passengers to pay more attention to Cuba. So disturbing was he to the peace that the waitress behind the counter finally said, "This is a business establishment. We don't want no trouble. Now get out." Out staggered the Cuban, and all went back to their pancakes and syrup, with the exception of a sailor, who just sat staring at his coffee. As the waitress went by he said, "Look, he wasn't trying to make you no trouble. He was trying to tell you you got trouble." But she only shrugged and

---

* William Sloane Coffin, Jr. is Chaplain at Yale University, and the two sermons here published were preached at Battell Chapel.

moved on. A few minutes later the sailor shoved away his coffee, untouched, put a dime on the counter, got up and said, "I don't like this place," and went out.

"We don't want no trouble." Famous words of Al Capone, expressing the feelings of people by the thousands who want peace at any price, so long as the peace is theirs and the price is paid by someone else. The church has been as guilty of this attitude as any business establishment. But the church is Christian when its ministers remember the injunction of Jeremiah not to "cry peace where there is no peace," and its people remember the startling words of their Lord, "I came not to bring peace but the sword." The Holy Spirit, let us never forget, comes not only as the comforter but as the discomforter.

One surely does not have to be a Christian, however, only a human being with his eyes open, to see that in this lunatic and bloody-minded age we "got trouble"; not normal trouble, either, not the normal "human madness" viewed by Zedekiah and Jeremiah, but the kind of trouble reflected in modern art, which first distorted the image of man, then broke it up and then caused it to disappear altogether. Art is prophetic, and here the prophecy is not the one as old as Jeremiah that men may one day lose their souls, but that one day men may have no souls to lose.

When one climbs the ramparts of this nation and looks at the dehumanizing consequences of totalitarianism outside and the dehumanizing consequences of a mass technical civilization inside, and considers the possibility that conflict between the two may mean the annihilation of the whole world, then who can deny that for the first time in human history the very humanity of human beings is at stake? "We got deep trouble." The human predicament is acute because it is at the level of meaning itself. I hope we can all agree that there is no more important question in human life than the question of meaning, so let us talk this morning about meaning.

Increasingly I think it is becoming apparent that as in the realm of physics so in the realm of human psychology a vacuum is just intolerable. Increasingly I think it is becoming apparent that man is not dominated by the will-to-pleasure, not dominated by the will-to-power, but dominated by a longing and a striving to find a more ultimate meaning to his life, dominated by a "will-to-meaning." Nietzsche foresaw this when he said, "If a man has a why for his life he can bear with almost any how." And Camus has again spoken for our age. "Here is what frightens me," says Cherea in *Caligula,* "to lose one's life is a little thing, and I will have the courage when necessary. But to see the sense of this life dissipated, to see our reason for existence disappear, that is what is intolerable. A man cannot live without meaning."

How many of us here today will experience that Sunday neurosis, that sense of the inner void, the lack of content in our lives once the rush of the busy week is over?

But where is meaning to be found? German existentialist philosophers these days are fond of talking of *Grenzsituationen,* that is, borderline or ultimate situations in human life which, unlike other situations in our lives, cannot be eliminated or changed; they can only be acknowledged. I must die. I must suffer. I must struggle. I am at the mercy of chance. I am inexorably involved in guilt. Now to search for meaning outside of these ultimate situations is obviously a complete waste of time. In a book entitled *From Death Camp to Existentialism,* Victor Frankl, who endured the worst of Nazi horrors, writes that while for most of the inmates the question of meaning hinged on the question of survival, for him meaning had to be affirmed in the context of no survival. "Has all this suffering, this dying around us, a meaning? For, if not, then ultimately there is no meaning to survival; for a life whose meaning stands and falls on whether one escapes with it or not—a life whose meaning depends upon such a happenstance—ultimately would not be worth living at all."

Frankl is a modern Socrates, in that it was Socrates who said, "To philosophize is to learn how to die." These two knew where to look for meaning. Many students these days find the experience of higher education rather meaningless. Why not? How many philosophers today consider death the burning business of philosophy? How many educators of all kinds consider the great implacabilities of human life, death and suffering, fate and sin, worthy of study? Why, most are paid to avoid these issues, as we educate not to make a life but to make a living. And of those not paid, don't the majority of educators, yes, right here at Yale, sidestep the ultimate realities of life with an agility that is positively breath-taking? Small wonder, then, higher education is not more meaningful. Small wonder that higher education paradoxically has never enjoyed a level of performance so high and a level of influence so low, influence on students of a nation which as a whole knows even less than its educators where to look for meaning. We Americans, as someone has recently said, are "Hamlets in supermarkets."

Meaning that has any validity must be able to give an answer to the question of death and suffering, fate and sin. The ultimate situations of life demand an ultimate answer. So, as every thinking atheist knows, either this world is finally meaningless, or there *is* a Word from the Lord.

But to whom is the Word of the Lord spoken? The answer I think is, to man, by which I mean not a man being a scientist, anthropologist or historian, but to a scientist, anthropologist or historian being a man. For the Word of God is not total knowledge given to man, but knowledge given to total man.

What do we mean by total man? More and more these days we seem to be considering man only as an object of inquiry, as a racial type for an ethnologist, a creature who produces by his labor for a Marxist, or one with unconscious drives for a psychologist. While all these inquiries usually produce something of interest, they never—their frequent claims to the contrary—describe man as a whole, for "total" man is a creature endowed with a freedom that is inaccessible to inquiry. The very freedom that leads man to inquire, "What is man?"—the same freedom precludes the possibility of a final answer. Man is, in short, more than he can know about himself for the fundamental reason that his freedom is not the object but the source of his thought.

Total man is unknowable, but if we cannot know ourselves we can experience ourselves in our totality, and this we do less when we think, more when we decide, and most intensely when with heart and mind and soul we decide what to do with our lives, given the ultimate realities of our existence.

Now a man being an intellectual is not a total man, for as an intellectual he is reflective but not necessarily decisive, and for this reason it is so hard for an intellectual to hear a Word from the Lord. He is just not prepared to. The other day I read of a new course in the Political Science Department of Northwestern, a course on "Decision Making." That course could be well taught by the most indecisive man on the Northwestern faculty, for to describe the actions of others it is not necessary to decide on one's own. But the Word of the Lord comes only to those who are ready to make a decision. Included in Jeremiah's category of those who "have ears and hear not" are those intellectuals determined to live in a state of suspended judgment.

Again, not the intellectual being a man, but the man being an intellectual has another handicap. The three steps we have been discussing—the ultimate situations in human life, the Word from the Lord, total man—all lie beyond the understandable. Now the intellectual is one who is proud of his intellectual penetration, and therefore one who has a hard time being humble before impenetrable mysteries. He is constantly tempted to believe that while there are things unknown there is nothing finally unknowable. Yet this belief, held of course on blind faith, is ironically the greatest threat to human freedom, the greatest threat to the humanity of human beings. For those who consider man a completely unknowable object inevitably must consider him as just another thing among the things he produces. Strange, isn't it, that intellectuals should constitute the greatest menace to human freedom!

Nicholas de Cusa said, "The intellect is a whore, for it can prostitute itself to anything." Actually it can prostitute itself only to human pride, and the intellectual community is no more immune from pride than any other. Actually you know there are people who think we are more virtuous. What they do not realize is that ours is a pseudo virtue, the virtue of being virtuous where we can afford to be. Do you remember Mark Twain's comment on how wonderful it was to be a Christian when you held all four aces in your hand? But to hear the Word of the Lord the intellectual must be willing to be total man, and willing to be modest, for as regards ultimate meaning our minds may play a legislative but not finally a creative role.

Now, finally, what does the Word of the Lord say? "I will give them a heart that they may know me." There is knowledge that is the fruit of reason, and there is also knowledge that is the fruit of love. While the Greeks sought the universe through reason, Jeremiah and the prophets sought the universe through a moral consciousness. The Greeks experienced the sovereignty of logic; the Israelites experienced the extraordinary universal sovereignty of righteousness. The Word of the Lord came to them as great universal ethical imperatives that carried intuitive conviction. They did not know with absolute intellectual certainty, but they knew with deep psychological certitude that meaning in human life was to be found in its moral dimension, that love not logic was the clue to reality. And this was a truth they did not possess. Rather, they were possessed by it.

The day before yesterday I spent several hours in the Fulton County jail in Atlanta, Georgia, with eighty-two Negro students jailed for instigating sit-in demonstrations. At their request their chaplain celebrated the sacrament of the Lord's Supper. In the waiting room outside the water came from drinking fountains labeled "Colored" and "White," but behind the bars the wine came to all of us from a common cup. The wrongness of the one and the rightness of the other were quite overpowering. "This is my body, broken for you. This is my blood, shed for you." Somehow in that moment in the crowded cell all the sin and suffering of Atlanta, the South, the nation, and even the world seemed reconciled in the sure knowledge of a God who "so loved the world that he gave his only begotten son that whosoever should believe in him should not perish but have eternal life."

There was a Word from the Lord. And the Word was love.

The Call

by William Sloane Coffin, Jr.

(Scripture: "When the Lord saw that he turned aside
to see, God called to him . . . 'Moses, Moses,' and he
said, 'Here am I.'" Exod. 3:4; "We know that we have
passed out of death into life, because we love the brethren." I John 3:14)

Reading the other day that excellent magazine, *The Christian Century,* I came across two items which seemed to reflect the two diametrically opposed types of religion now
vying in this country to represent Christianity. The first
item was a review of a book just out whose title probably
indicates that popular piety has just hit an all-time low. The
book is called, *I Prayed Myself Slim,* but according to the
reviewer a better title might be "The Power of Positive
Shrinking." Apparently the young authoress, having gal-
vanized her gumption and gotten God on her side, carried
through on a crash diet, and in ten months' time was eighty-
two pounds lighter and for the first time in her life having
dates, dates, dates. She even got invited to the Governor's

Inaugural Ball, where, praise be to God, she was no longer a waddling wallflower!

However, the book is not without its merits for those of you who find yourselves, as did Miss Pierce, in the dark and lonely abyss of gluttony. Here you can find helpful luncheon hints on how to nibble celery stalks and carrot tips while sipping two glasses of cold water.

But I cite the book not for the benefit of those of you who cast inelegant shadows but for one singularly illustrative feature. Out of some fifty-eight prayers offered by Miss Pierce only four acknowledge the existence of other people.

Although the book as a whole might make even Mr. Peale wince, this feature seems typical of the incredible self-centeredness of today's popular piety. Historically, of course, piety has rarely had much to do with morality, but today so little that the managing editor of *The Christian Century* can argue persuasively that the so-called religious revival in this country is actually contributing to the national moral decay. How often we are told what God can do for us; how rarely what God can do with us! God, no longer the cosmic policeman of the fiery furnace religion, is now a sort of cosmic bellhop, ready to do anything to make life pleasant and safe without asking for anything more than a reasonable tip. In Old Testament days, as you remember, Samuel prayed, "Speak, Lord, for thy servant heareth," but how many today pray, "Listen, Lord, for thy servant speaketh. Thou must give unto me a good job, a nice family, a fine set of principles—accent on flexibility, of course—and most of all peace, O Lord, a peace that nothing can disturb." Occasionally, this type of prayer has a P.S., "O yes, Lord, I have done wrong but please don't let anyone find out. And one more thing: Help me to spread a little happiness as I pass along—so that I can keep my self-esteem."

Thus it was a real pleasure to read an entirely different type of prayer, a prayer by the first layman President of the National Council of Churches, and if provincial pride be permitted, a member of the Yale Corporation. Last month in his installation services as President of the Council Mr. J. Irwin Miller prayed: "O Father . . . we have presumed upon thy patience. . . . We pray now, O Father, to be used roughly."

At the beginning of a new year and a new decade, not to mention a new national Administration, now perhaps is a good time for all of us to decide again in which of these two religious camps we want to try to be; a good time to realize again that Christianity is tender, yes, but tough, appealing but frightening, comforting but also impossibly difficult. For Christianity is not some vague atmosphere, spiritual climate, or glow in the heart, but an allegiance to a demanding relationship, one, we might say, that must be re-established every day. I believe it was Renan who said, "Democracy is a daily plebiscite." Likewise, Christianity must be chosen daily, and we do so whenever in the cataclysmic events of our time or in the humble events of daily life we hear, "Moses, Moses," and can bring ourselves to answer, "Here am I."

One doesn't hear much about the "call" of God these days. For instance, of the two thousand students at Yale now job hunting for next June or September few are consciously

listening for any "call" of God. Most are listening instead to
the advice of their friends, which for the most part is just
appalling. "Be realistic." "Use judgment." Why don't we
give it to them straight: "Don't go out on a limb; cling to
the trunk; look out for every bit of self-advantage you can
get." Have we nothing better to offer ourselves? Do you remember the prayer of the old French Marshal, "God save
me from my friends. I can protect myself from my enemies."? But a few students are seriously trying to hear
God calling, and it is they who have stimulated these
thoughts. The subject of calling is obviously so wide and
subtle I can only hope to suggest one often forgotten way in
which I believe God calls each of us.

Contrary to the popular notion, I think God usually calls
us not directly—we can manipulate that call too easily—but
indirectly through other people, and the call comes in some
such fashion as this. Have you even been to an old vaudeville show? There are not many left, but inevitably they in-
clude a magician whose patter is almost always the same.
He starts with one about the dentist and the manicurist who
got married and spent the rest of their lives fighting tooth
and nail. Then he says, "You should show more respect for
my jokes, they're older than you are. My act is terrific: it
not only answers the question who killed vaudeville, but re-
enacts the crime before your eyes." And everybody sits back
to enjoy what to me at least is wonderful "corn." Then suddenly he stops. "Will the gentleman in the end seat please
come forward?" You look around to see whom he has got
this time, but you hear him say, "No, not you, the gentle-

man turning around," and to your horror you realize he means you. You're furious. You didn't pay your money for this. You paid to be a spectator, and now this fellow is calling you to take part in the act.

But are you furious, or let's say annoyed, because the call is a call to action? In part yes, because I think fundamentally most of us really would like nothing better in this world than to purchase a life membership in the Association of Bystanders. More annoying, however, is that by making an unforeseen demand upon you, this call robs you of the initiative in action, that is, it threatens your freedom; but worst of all the call places you under judgment, for in the response you make will be revealed the kind of person you are.

What the call of the magician does to us is in a superficial way what other people are doing to us all the time, and some in a very profound and hence far more annoying way. Sartre, then, is right when he says the other person can only be viewed in terms of discomfort; right when he has one of his characters cry out, "Hell, that's other people!" For other people really have only to present themselves and we are already under judgment, for the response we make— and no response is a response—reveals the kind of person we are. The presence of another, then, constitutes a call to self-revelation, a call to action, yes, but more fundamentally a call *into being,* for in Jasper's famous phrase, "I am through the other."

But who am I? Moses' first question to God. When we talk of the nature of men we do not mean men are alike in terms of finished products. We mean they are alike in terms, if you will, of the basic raw materials to be found in their make-up, for we all have certain similar physical and psychological needs, and, from a Christian point of view, alike in terms of an ultimate goal. Man is not as he eats, not as he thinks, man is as he loves. From a Christian point of view there is no smaller package in this world than a man all wrapped up in himself. From a Christian point of view a man becomes a man only as he develops his capacity to love, for as the letter of John describes the process of becoming, "We pass out of death into life because we love the brethren."

What man is essentially, however, he is never existentially. The call we receive, then, has as its main purpose to bring these two states of being into closer correlation. But we are perverse. We want to come into being, and yet we do not, and so it is, I think, that to move us the call to love usually must come from those who need love most.

Most of us here have taken the train to New York. Going through Fairfield and Westchester Counties it is easy, isn't it, to remain a spectator. But after the 125th Street station, when you look out the window at that "island in the city," as the Puerto Rican district is called, when you look at all that frustrated truncated human life, don't you feel you are being placed in judgment? Aren't you really relieved when, instead of all those Puerto Rican faces you suddenly see your own reflected in the window as the train enters the tunnel?

We say we hate to see suffering, but is it the suffering or the sufferers we hate? I shall never forget my first conscious experience of hating sufferers. It was in 1945, and we were ordered to repatriate forcefully a camp full of Soviet soldiers and officers captured by the Germans who just did not want to go back to the Soviet Union. I shall never forget the look in their eyes, particularly in the eyes of those we had to cut down from the ceiling where they were hanging themselves by their own bootstraps. And I shall never forget how we hated them for making us hate ourselves. And something of the same look was in the eyes of all those bodies piled up at Dachau, eyes that still seemed to live, though the bodies were days dead; and in the eyes of the twenty million DP's for whom we as Americans did next to nothing; and today it is the children in New Orleans and the seventy dispossessed Negro sharecroppers in Fayette County, Tennessee, the Algerians, the Laotians, and the lonely and the mixed-up in our midst—all these sufferers placing us under judgment, calling us into being, calling us to love, calling us to suffer with them, for what is love if not the willingness and capacity to suffer?

I firmly believe God is calling us daily into being, and calling us primarily through the sufferers of this world. How else can one interpret the story of Moses; Moses, who even among the sheep of his father-in-law in the faraway wilderness by Horeb still could not forget the voices of his people, until finally one day through them he heard the voice of God Himself, "I have seen the affliction of my people. I know their sufferings, and I have come down to deliver them. Come, I will send you." All those conspicuously called in the Bible—Moses, Samuel, Saul, David, Amos, Jere-

miah, Isaiah, and all the disciples and apostles—all were
called in relationship to the affliction of their people. Why,
then, should the call be different for us? And why should
we think the answer was any easier for them? They didn't
just fall on their knees before God. They reared up on their
hind legs, "Why me?" "I don't want to go to Pharaoh, to
Ahab, to Zedekiah." But they did, not confident of their
own ability, not confident even of success, but confident only
that God would make good his promise, "I will be with
you."

I am glad we are celebrating Communion today, for this
sacrament re-enacts this very promise of God. The sacrament is also, of course, a direct call of God—this is my body,
broken for you—a call from God's suffering son to suffer
with him for others. The church needs this sacrament, for
in our country by and large the church has lost its capacity
to suffer. The religious revival is superficial precisely because
it has so little understanding of suffering.

"We pray now, O Father, to be used roughly." Do we
mean it? Are we willing to be placed under judgment, to be
called into being? In the cataclysmic event of the new year
and decade, and in the humble events of our daily lives,
wherever there is need for love are we willing to hear,
"Moses, Moses"? If so, God grant us grace to reply, "Here
am I," for "We pass out of death into life because we love
the brethren." Now let us pray the entire prayer of Mr.
Miller.

"FATHER OF us all, we have taken advantage of Thy great and un-
qualified love. We have presumed upon Thy patience to do less than

we might have done, to have been timid where we should have shown courage, to have been careful where we should have been reckless, not counting the cost. We pray now, O Father, to be used roughly. Stamp on our selfishness. Chill our warm and comfortable content with things as they are. Frighten us with an awareness of our new power to destroy ourselves and frustrate Thy purpose for Thy children. Open our eyes to the opportunities for great and marvelous achievement which lie at our hands. And fill us with urgency and zeal to accomplish what we have in us to do in the years which have been provided us. In Jesus' name. AMEN."

The Care of the Earth

by Joseph Sittler *

(Scripture: Psalm 104)

A sermon may move from idea to fulfillment in various, and sometimes strange, ways. It may be useful as an introduction to the theme of this sermon to say how that happened in the writing of it.

In April of last year I read a poem in *The New Yorker* magazine; the poet is Mr. Richard Wilbur. What the poet was saying struck and stuck for several obvious reasons. Beneath the quite clear apprehensions that float about just under the surface of our minds there is a root-apprehension that churns deep down at the center. It is vague; but it is also relentless and undismissable. And the poet's words interest this inarticulate anxiety, stop it cold, give it a "local habitation and a name." The substance of this anxiety is common to us all; and it is heavy. It is the peculiar function of the poet sometimes to say out loud and with resonant

* Joseph Sittler is Professor in the Divinity School of the University of Chicago. This sermon was preached at the Eisenhower Chapel, Pennsylvania State University.

clarity what we all would wish to say had we the dark music and the language.

The substance is this: annihilating power is in nervous and passionate hands. The stuff is really there to incinerate the earth—and the certainty that it will not be used is not there.

Nor have we anodyne to hush it up or power to run away from it. We can go skiing with it, trot off to Bermuda with it, push it down under accelerated occupation with the daily round, pour bourbon over it, or say our prayers—each according to his tactic and disposition. But it goes along, survives, talks back.

Not in abstract propositions or dramatic warnings but in powerful, earthy images the poet makes his point. The point is single, simple, and absolute: man's selfhood hangs upon the persistence of the earth, her dear known and remembered factualness is the matrix of the self.

ADVICE TO A PROPHET

When you come, as you soon must, to the streets of our city,
Mad-eyed from stating the obvious,
Not proclaiming our fall but begging us
In God's name to have self-pity,

Spare us all word of the weapons, their force and range,
The long numbers that rocket the mind;
Our slow, unreckoning hearts will be left behind,
Unable to fear what is too strange.

Nor shall you scare us with talk of the death of the race.
How should we dream of this place without us—
The sun mere fire, the leaves untroubled about us,
A stone look on the stone's face?

Speak of the world's own change. Though we cannot conceive
Of an undreamt thing, we know to our cost
How the dreamt cloud crumbles, the vines are blackened by frost,
How the view alters. We could believe,

If you told us so, that the white-tailed deer will slip
Into perfect shade, grown perfectly shy,
The lark avoid the reaches of our eye,
The jack-pine lose its knuckled grip

On the cold ledge, and every torrent burn
As Xanthus once, its gliding trout
Stunned in a twinkling. What should we be without
The dolphin's arc, the dove's return,

These things in which we have seen ourselves and spoken?
Ask us, prophet, how we shall call
Our natures forth when that live tongue is all
Dispelled, that glass obscured or broken,

In which we have said the rose of our love and the clean
Horse of our courage, in which beheld
The singing locust of the soul unshelled,
And all we mean or wish to mean.

Ask us, ask us whether with the wordless rose
Our hearts shall fail us; come demanding
Whether there shall be lofty or long standing
When the bronze annals of the oak-tree close.[1]

By the sheer force of these lines my mind was pushed back against the wall and forced to ask: is there anything in our Western religious tradition as diagnostically penetrating as that problem, as salvatory as that predicament?

Out of these back-to-wall reflections I therefore ask your attention to several statements that seem to me alone deep

[1] Richard Wilbur, "Advice to a Prophet," published in *The New Yorker* (April 4, 1959). Reprinted from his volume, *Advice to a Prophet and Other Poems* by permission of Harcourt, Brace & World, Inc.

and strong enough to make adequate sense. These statements have in common this: they deal with the enjoyment of things and the uses of things. And together they add up to a proposition: delight is the basis of right use.

The first statement is the celebrated answer to the first question in the Westminster catechism. No one will question the velocity with which this answer gets to the point or that the point is worth getting at! The question is: What is the chief end of man? The answer: To glorify God and enjoy Him forever!

The first verb, "to glorify," is not primarily intellectual. It does *not concern* itself with the establishment of the existence of God, or with a description of His nature. The verb is not aesthetic, either. It is not concerned to declare that God is good or beautiful, or propose that it is a fair thing to worship God. Nor is it hortatory; that is, it does not beat us over the head with admonitions about our duty to God.

The verb "to glorify" is exclusively and utterly religious! The verb comes from the substantive "glory": and that term designates what God is and has and wills within Himself; it announces the priority, the ineffable majesty, the sovereign power and freedom of the Holy. To glorify, that is to say, is what God is and does out of Himself; and when we use the term for what we do in response, that response is given and engendered by His glory.

The priority-in-God, and the proper work of this verb may be illustrated by its function in the sixth chapter of the book of Isaiah. The young prophet, rich and eager in his expectations of the new king, Uzziah, is stunned when the king dies. He goes into the temple. And then comes the vision of the glory of whose ineffable power the face of the king is but the reflection.

> In the year that King Uzziah died I saw the Lord sitting upon a throne, high and lifted up; and his train filled the temple. Above him stood the seraphim: each had six wings: with two he covered his face, and with two he covered his feet, and with two he flew. And one called to another and said:
> "Holy, holy, holy is the LORD of
> hosts:
> the whole earth is full of his glory." (Isa. 6:1–3)

The glory is the light the Holy gives off. The earth is a theater of the glory; it is rich with the ineffable glory because God, the Holy one, has made it.

The Holy is a numinous and absolute word. It is not contained within other categories; it is a category. The Holy both evokes and demands thought, but it is a misunderstanding to assume that thoughts can contain the glory and the Holy. The Holy certainly has the effect that Professor Rudolph Otto in his great work *The Idea of the Holy* calls *mysterium tremendum et fascinocem*—but there is an unseizable plus to the term that eludes even the image-making genius of the Jews.

The Holy invites prayer; but rejects such an understanding of prayer as would make prayer a tool for working upon the Holy, a device for making the Holy disposable by man. The Holy demands service; but no service adds up to a responding equivalent—just as in our human love one serves the beloved but never affirms his service to be the measure of love.

The chief end of man is, then, to glorify God, to let God be God, to understand and accept his life in ways appropriate to the imperial, Holy singularity of God. The meaning of this has, to be sure, ethical, psychological, even political implications. But the center is categorically religious.

But this statement about God and man, thus elevated, tough, and absolute, is conjoined in the catechism with a concluding phrase, "and enjoy Him forever." The juxtaposition of commands "to glorify" and "to enjoy" is on several grounds startling to our generation. "To enjoy" is a strange thing, that is to say, to do about the Holy God before whom even the seraphim do hide their faces. This joining of the Holy, which is what God is, with joy, which designates what man is to have and do in Him—this juxtaposition, in that it is startling to us, says a good deal about modern American understanding of the Christian faith. How it has come about that we are startled by what our fathers joined together without batting an eye is a matter we cannot now go into—but only observe it and ask after its significance. For we may have missed something. If the gravity of the glorification of the Holy and the blithe humaneness of "enjoy Him forever" seem strange, our churches in the very form of their buildings may be partly to blame. There is the clean, shadowless, and antiseptic colonial, the monumental melancholy of the Romanesque and Gothic adaptations—bereft of the color and ornament which in other lands are so devoutly joined in these forms. Our traditional churches affirm a heavy kind of solemnity that leaves us indeed with a lugubrious Holy, but defenseless and aghast before the joy of, for instance, a

Baroque church. These are luxuriant, joy-breathing, positively Mozartean in their vivacity—replete with rosy angels tumbling in unabashed enjoyment among impossibly fleecy clouds against an incredibly blue heaven.

We shall not draw conclusions from that—only observe it and let it hang—that the gravity of a life determined by God, lived to the glory of God, is not necessarily incongruent with abounding joy. It is interesting to recall that the most rollicking organ music old periwig Bach ever wrote is not dedicated to the joy of tobacco (although he did that) or coffee (and he praised that) or the inventiveness among his fellow musicians, nor dedicated to the levity of the Count of Brandenburg—but *In Dir ist Freude* (In Thee is Joy)!

The second statement is ascribed to Thomas Aquinas, surely not the playful or superficial type. Thomas did not affirm Christianity as a consolatory escape hatch or an unguent to the scratchy personality or a morale-builder to a threatened republic—all contemporary malformations. But he did say, "It is of the heart of sin that men use what they ought to enjoy, and enjoy what they ought to use." Apart from the claim that it is sin that men do that, and apart from the seriousness of the situation if that statement should turn out to be true, is the statement reportorially so?

Yes—it is so—for all of us, and in many ways. Thomas is simply condensing here the profound dialectic of use and enjoyment that distorts and impoverishes life when it is not acknowledged and obeyed. To use a thing is to make it instrumental to a purpose; and some things are to be so used.

To enjoy a thing is to permit it to be what it is prior to and apart from any instrumental assessment of it—and some things are to be so enjoyed.

I adduce a small example: it may bloom in our minds into bigger ones. Wine is to be enjoyed; it is not to be used. Wine is old in human history. It is a symbol of nature in her smiling beneficence—"close bosom friend of the maturing sun." That is why it has virtually everywhere and always been the accompaniment of celebrative occasions, the sign of gladness of heart. It is to be enjoyed; it is not to be used to evoke illusions of magnificence, or stiffen timidity with the fleeting certainty that one is indeed a sterling lad. Where it is enjoyed it adds grace to truth; where it is used it induces and anesthetizes a lie.

Observe the 104th Psalm, how the Old Testament man who sought to glorify God and enjoy him forever stood in the midst of nature. "He giveth wine to gladden the heart of man, oil to make his face shine." "This is the day which the Lord hath made," he exults, "let us rejoice and be glad in it." (Ps. 118:24) Why? Not primarily for what he can turn the day's hours into. But rather the primal ground that there are days—unaccountable in their gift-character, just there. And here he is—permeable by all he is sensitive to, texture, light, form, and movement—the cattle on a thousand hills—Thou sendest forth thy Spirit and they are. Let us rejoice and be glad in it!

> i thank You God for most this amazing
> day:for the leaping greenly spirits of trees

and a blue true dream of sky;and for everything
which is natural which is infinite which is yes [2]

It is the heart of sin that man uses what he ought to enjoy.

It is also, says Thomas, of the heart of sin that man is content to enjoy what he ought to use. Charity, for instance. Charity is the comprehensive term to designate how God regards man. That regard is to be used by man for man. That is why our Lord moves always in his speech from the source of joy—that man is loved by the Holy—to the theater of joy —that man must serve the need of the neighbor. "Lord, where did we behold Thee? I was in prison, hungry, cold, naked"—you enjoyed a charity that God gives for use.

If the creation, including our fellow creatures, is impiously used apart from a gracious primeval joy in it, the very richness of the creation becomes a judgment. This has a cleansing and orderly meaning for everything in the world of nature—from the sewage we dump into our streams to the cosmic sewage we dump into the fallout.

Abuse is use without grace; it is always a failure in the counterpoint of use and enjoyment. When things are not used in ways determined by joy in the things themselves, this violated potentiality of joy (timid as all things Holy, but relentless and blunt in its reprisals)—withdraws and leaves us, not perhaps with immediate positive damnations, but with something much worse: the wan, ghastly, negative damnations of use without joy, stuff without grace, a busy,

[2] e. e. cummings, "i thank You God for most this amazing," reprinted from his volume, *Poems, 1923–1954,* by permission of Harcourt, Brace & World, Inc.

fabricating world with the shine gone off, personal relations for the nature of which we have invented the eloquent term "contacts," staring without beholding, even fornication without finding.

God is useful. But not if he is sought for use. Ivan, in *The Brothers Karamazov,* saw that, and Dostoevsky meant it as a witness to the Holy and joy-begetting God, whom he saw turned into an ecclesiastical club to frighten impoverished peasants with—when he had his character say, "I deny God for God's sake!"

All of this has, I think, something to say to us as teachers and students to whom this university is ever freshly available for enjoyment and use. For consider this: the basis of discovery is curiosity; and what is curiosity but the peculiar joy of the mind in its own given nature. Sheer curiosity, without immediate anticipation of ends and uses, has done most to envision new ends and fresh uses. But curiosity does this in virtue of a strange counterpoint of use and enjoyment. Bacon declared that "studies are for delight," the secular counterpart of, "Glorify God and enjoy Him forever." The Creator, who is the Fountain of Joy—and the creation, which is the material of university study—are here brought together in an ultimate way. It is significant that the university, the institutional solidification of the fact that studies are for delight, is an idea and a creation of a culture that once affirmed that men should glorify God and enjoy Him forever.

Use is blessed when enjoyment is honored. Piety is deepest practicality, for it properly relates use and enjoyment.

And a world sacramentally received in joy is a world sanely used. There is an economics of use only; it moves toward the destruction of both use and joy. And there is an economics of joy; it moves toward the intelligence of use, and the enhancement of joy. That this vision involves a radical new understanding of the clean and fruitful earth is certainly so. But this vision, deeply religious in its genesis, is not so very absurd now that natural damnation is in orbit, and man's befouling of his ancient home has spread his death and dirt among the stars.

The Strangeness of Faith

by Will Herberg *

(Scripture: "I know your works; you are neither cold nor
hot. Would that you were cold or hot! So, because you
are lukewarm, and neither cold nor hot, I will spew you
out of my mouth." Rev. 3:15–16)

I preach today on a text from Martin Luther who so well
understood the strangeness of faith. "I will say one thing
boldly and freely," Luther once declared. "Nobody in this
life is nearer to God than those who hate and deny him, and
he has no more pleasing, no more dear children than these."
What shall we make of this astounding statement? What
could Luther conceivably have meant by such an incredible
assertion: no one in this life nearer to God, no one dearer to
him, than those who hate and deny him? Shall we charge it
to Luther's notorious fondness for utterances violent and extreme, or does this paradox reveal something profound about
the meaning of faith that we in our conventional piety tend
to overlook?

* Will Herberg is Professor at Drew University. This sermon was
preached in chapel services at Emory University and elsewhere and is
reprinted from *The Pulpit* by permission.

I think that perhaps the latter is the case. Luther's statement, however shocking and extreme it may sound, seems to me to point to a profound truth that lies at the very heart of authentic faith: that unless God matters infinitely, he does not matter at all. There is something absolute about faith which demands everything or nothing. Faith is not just one more interest or attachment in life, side by side with other interests and attachments; if it were merely that, it would indeed be nothing at all. "Faith," the great Jewish philosopher Martin Buber has said, "is not a feeling in the soul, but an entrance into reality, an entrance into the whole reality without reduction or curtailment." If it is genuine, it is everything; it touches everything and transforms everything, and when it is thrown into question, everything is thrown into question: all life is at stake.

That is what Luther is saying. The passionate unbeliever who "hates" and "denies" God may be all wrong in his ideas, but at least he takes God seriously. This kind of unbeliever is no mere unbeliever; he is rather an antibeliever whose whole life is a wrestling with God, whose whole mind is preoccupied with the problem of faith. Whatever else he may do, he does not take God for granted; he does not commit the ultimate sin of indifference. For that reason, Luther insists, he is near to God and dear to him.

The Ultimate Sin

Not unbelief but indifference, not atheism but taking God for granted, is the ultimate sin. Let me put it another way: not skeptical questioning, not even passionate denial of

God, is so displeasing to him as the lukewarmness of conventional piety. This is what Luther is saying; and in saying this he is merely echoing the searing words with which the Bible denounces the lukewarm in faith. Very few people nowadays read that strange book that comes at the end of the New Testament, the Book of Revelation; but we miss a great deal in overlooking it. For it is filled with the burning passion of faith which kindles the imagination, despite the grotesque and often weird imagery in which it is expressed. There are those unforgettable chapters in which the seven churches in Asia are described by means of "letters" addressed to their "angels" or spiritual leaders. To the church in Laodicea the Almighty dictates the following message: "I know your works; you are neither cold nor hot. Would that you were cold or hot! So, because you are lukewarm, and neither cold nor hot, I will spew you out of my mouth." We all belong to this church of Laodicea, the church of the lukewarm; so let us take these words to heart. God can forgive anything but he cannot forgive mediocrity. Those who are mediocre in faith—neither hot nor cold but lukewarm—he spews forth.

Friedrich Nietzsche, the German philosopher, had his mixed feelings about the New Testament, but this passage at least he must have understood and approved. For Nietzsche the atheist was infuriated at the utter insipidity of so much of the Christianity of his time. Mockingly, passionately, he denounced its stodginess, its superficiality, its sentimentalism; with blinding anger he exposed the degradation of the faith into a conventional sanctification of conventional mediocrity. Who today takes God seriously? he demanded; and because he looked and looked and could find no one in whatever direction he turned, he proclaimed defiantly that God was "dead." He was wrong; God was not "dead"; what was dead was the faith of the conventional piety that had so degraded God. Yet, in his error Nietzsche was surely less distant from God's truth than were the conventional believers who so self-righteously denounced him: he took God seriously; they took him for granted.

Atheism: Faith Inverted

Where do we find our Nietzsches today? We have none and we are much the poorer for their absence. On one campus where I have spent a good deal of time there was an old professor now retired, a man of great eminence in his field. Whenever anyone spoke to me about him, it was always with an indulgent smile: "He's our campus atheist," they would say; "don't take him too seriously." Yet I learned to take him seriously enough, for he took with the utmost seriousness the questions I was there to discuss. He attended all the lectures and meetings, even the chapel service, raised every conceivable objection, and threw himself heart and soul into the controversy. The topics we discussed meant much to him, as one could readily see from his eagerness and excitement. Yes, he was an "atheist"; but he was obsessed, literally obsessed, with the things of God. His more religious colleagues dismissed him, together with his atheism, as a leftover from an age past and gone, as indeed he was. But I am afraid that some of them were as much perplexed by the passion of his concern as by his atheistic opinions. They could not see that his passion was the passion of faith curiously inverted; his very denial of God was, strangely enough, a testimony to God's reality and power. They, the more conventionally pious, had in their very piety lost the almost feverish sense of excitement at things divine which the old man, for all his atheism—perhaps even because of his atheism—still retained.

Luther would have known what to make of this man, as he would have known what to make of Friedrich Nietzsche, the man who scandalized the world of his time by proclaiming that God was dead. Luther understood men like these; he opposed them but he understood them. What infuriated Luther was not passionate doubt or denial but conventional piety. In uttering his paradoxical words about the God-denier who is near to God, Luther was denouncing the conventional piety of the good, self-satisfied Christians in the pews, and attempting to shock them into a sense of their condition. For the condition of the good, self-satisfied Christian, of the religious man of conventional piety, is a perilous one indeed. He has put God in his place, somewhere on the margin of life, where he permits him to occupy a very honorable position but also a very innocuous one. Conventional piety issues no challenge and makes no demand; it merely reassures the church member that all is well with him because he, after all, is on the inside of the church, engaged in pious works and exercises, while the unbeliever is on the outside in outer darkness. In this way conventional piety tends to confirm man in his self-righteousness and good opinion of himself; indeed, it often actually supplies him with another device by which these may be sanctioned in the name of religion. (For there is something strangely ambiguous about religion. It is, on the one side, man's openness to the divine, but on the other side, it is always being converted into a means of spiritual self-sufficiency, which shuts one off from God.) Religion and church membership may thus well become a kind of defense that the conventionally religious man throws up to protect himself against the absolute demand of faith. That is why the great Christian theologian (Karl Barth is always warning us that "the church is not only the place where man meets God; it is often also the place where man makes his last stand against God." How? By using religion and church membership to bolster his self-complacency.) When that happens, the witness of the passionate unbeliever, who takes his unbelief and therefore God seriously, becomes a witness to God. For it is a challenge to a religion that has become detestable to God because it has become a routine, conventional cult of reassurance.

A Much-Needed Witness

The witness of the passionate unbeliever to the seriousness of faith and the all-importance of God is a witness that men have needed at all times, but at no time perhaps more than today. For today, with the boom in religion under way in this country, we are in danger of being stifled by a heavy blanket of conventional religiosity as superficial and shoddy as anything known in history. Everybody is religious, and religion is everywhere, but it is a religion that is little more than a celebration of the values of our culture and a way of achieving "peace of mind" and the "power of positive thinking" in a situation where it is rather "divine discontent" and an unblinking confrontation of the hard facts of life that are required. Contemporary American religiosity is converting God into a great cosmic public utility which we find useful in advancing our purposes as individuals and as a nation. We have appointed God to his place in our scheme of things, and we are sure that since we are "religious" he will not fail us in the duties we have assigned to him. Having settled that little detail, we can go on to the things that really count, the things that John Wesley was wont to describe as the "pride and desire of life," in other words, the things through which we can display to all the world our success and superiority. No wonder that over half of the American people who say that they regard religion as a "very important thing" also readily admit that their religious beliefs have little or nothing to do with their ideas on economics or politics or other concerns of everyday life. Our lives we fashion on other grounds and other principles, and then we look to God, if we look to him at all, to certify our values and guarantee their success.

A Challenge to Complacency

It is here that the unbeliever utters his word of denial as a challenge to our complacency. Are we really so sure of God as we like to believe? Note that here the unbeliever with his questioning, and the prophet with his word of judg-

ment and wrath, join in shattering the false securities we
have built up in the name of religion. It is indeed sometimes
not easy to tell them apart, the prophet and the unbeliever.
That great Christian thinker Soren Kierkegaard, to whom
we owe so much of contemporary religious philosophy,
ended his brief and stormy life with a series of writings
which he called Attack Upon Christendom. By "Christendom" Kierkegaard meant the established, conventional
Christianity of his time. What he found so repulsive in it was
the all-pervading, though unconscious, hypocrisy in which
it was involved: the Christian faith in all its ultimacy was
indeed affirmed, but life continued to be lived on the comfortable level of human self-sufficiency. Whatever else he
could tolerate, this was one thing Kierkegaard could not
stand, and he lashed out at it with all the scorn and fury at
his command. No wonder so many of the scandalized
churchmen of his time put him down as an atheist, a mad-
man, or both! How could one claim to be religious and yet
say such horrible things about religion!

If Kierkegaard is the God-possessed prophet who speaks
words that make him sound like an atheist, Freud, like
Nietzsche, is the atheist who speaks words that have their
prophetic ring. Freud, as we all know, was hostile to religion; but then much of what he took for religion was sham
and deserved his hostility. Above all, Freud hated sham. He
had a truly Kierkegaardian contempt for those who were
trying to win favor for religion by presenting it under false
colors so as to deprive it of its "scandal" and challenge. In
the midst of one of his diatribes against religion, he breaks

out with these impassioned words: "One would like to count oneself among the believers so as to be able to admonish the philosophers who try to preserve the God of religion by substituting for him an impersonal, shadowy, abstract principle, and say to them: 'Thou shalt not take the name of the Lord thy God in vain!' " In these words Freud the atheist stands at the verge of the faith he denied; and we who espouse this faith can recognize in him, despite himself, a witness to the God of Truth we serve.

Obsessed with God

Yes, the God-obsessed God-affirmer and God-obsessed God-denier have something in common that we do not always estimate at its true worth. Both insist on ruthlessly tearing away the false securities we build up in the name of religion and forcing us to confront God and his absolute demand face to face—the prophet out of the passion of faith, the unbeliever out of the passion of doubt, but both out of the passion of infinite concern. It is this infinite concern that is at the heart of the matter. Where that is present, even though in negative form, there is nearness to God; where that is absent, nothing remains.

I do not want to disparage the importance of right belief in the life of faith. It is both central and indispensable, for right belief in matters of faith is essentially a right understanding of one's existence and a right direction to one's life. Nor do I want to minimize the gross errors in matters of belief committed by Nietzsche, Freud and the other unbelievers of whom I have spoken. Nietzsche's views on Christianity were perverse and often incoherent; Freud's views on religion were something of which not even his most devoted disciples are particularly proud. We need not mince words: Freud's philosophical outlook was shallow and crude, his understanding of the Jewish and Christian religions embarrassingly superficial, and his venture into the formal critique of religion a lamentable blunder. The explicit teachings of these men as they deal with religion are often dangerously misleading and have misled many fine minds. This we cannot overlook or excuse. And yet—for there is a "yet" —and yet it is not the last word. Luther was surely not unaware that the teachings of those who "hate and deny" God were false and blasphemous (he even uses this very word "blasphemous"); yet he also understood that for all their grievous error, they were performing a service on behalf of the truth and the God of Truth: they were denouncing spiritual sham and calling to spiritual authenticity, even if the true nature of this authenticity was hidden from them. Because this was what they were doing, Luther was bold enough to assert that they were "near and dear" to God.

Luther was a great man of God and a great theologian. He saw the perils of false belief, but he also saw the perils of conventional religion. He had the courage to state the paradoxes of faith in opposition to conventional piety with the whole force of his being. Speaking thus, Luther spoke in a great tradition, stretching all the way from the prophets of Israel to the so-called "religious existentialists" of today. And just as Luther dared to say that "nobody in this life is nearer to God than those who hate and deny him," so today we should have the courage to consider the possibility that unreligious, even antireligious poets,)novelists and philosophers may have more to say to us about the deepest problems of faith than those who drone out the pious platitudes of conventional religion, or those who try to convert these platitudes into a cheery, self-serving gospel of "peace of mind" and "positive thinking." There is a deeper and more genuine understanding of the religious dimension of life, it seems to me, in an "existentialist" novel such as *The Plague* or *The Fall* by Albert Camus than in all the exhortations of the professional purveyors of the gospel of reassurance put together. (But was not Camus an atheist? Perhaps, but he was an atheist concerned—one might almost say obsessed—with the ultimate problems of human life and therefore with God, though it is a God he did not know, while the conventional representatives of religion seem to be concerned mainly with "being religious," which almost leaves God out of the picture.)

It is this concern that is decisive one way or the other. The one unforgivable sin, let me remind you, is lukewarmness, mediocrity, taking God for granted. The man of faith, in his passionate concern with the ultimate, is sometimes less distant from Luther's "God-denier" than he is from the conventional believer, precisely because the former is passionately concerned with the ultimate and the latter is not.) Luther understood this very well; so did the eighteenth-century Jewish teacher, Nahman of Bratslav. One day a man came to Rabbi Nahman defiantly yet anxiously proclaiming that he did not believe in God. "So," said Rabbi Nahman,

"you don't believe in God; why get so excited about it? If God does not exist, it can't be very important, can it?" "But, Rabbi," the unbeliever expostulated, "how can you talk that way? It *is* important; it's the most important thing in the world." "Then, my son," said Rabbi Nahman, "you need not despair: though far from God, you are near to him.")
(Martin Luther and Nahman of Bratslav: they understood the meaning of faith.)

On Betrayal and Trust

by B. Davie Napier *

(Scripture: Psalm 8; Gen. 12:1 and 15:6; Isa. 7:9b)

There are three very brief items I must set out here before we begin. One is the Old Testament historian's interpretation of the Call of Abraham:

Now the Lord said to Abram, "Go from your country and your kindred and your father's house to the land that I will show you."

The second item appears a few chapters later in Genesis:

And [Abraham] believed the Lord, and [the Lord] reckoned it to him—[that is attributed the quality of belief to him]—as righteousness.

The third is a comparable statement from the prophet Isaiah to the king of Jerusalem and Judah in the eighth century B.C.

If you will not believe [said the prophet], surely you shall not be established.

* B. Davie Napier is Professor in Yale Divinity School.

In the novel by William Styron entitled *Set This House On Fire*,* the character Peter Leverett speaks of a period in his life when he says:

"I had incessant dreams of treachery and betrayal—dreams that lingered all day long. One of them especially I remember; like most fierce nightmares it had the habit of coming back again and again. In this one I was in a house somewhere, trying to sleep; it was dead of night, wintry and storming. Suddenly I heard a noise at the window, a sinister sound, distinct from the tumult of the rain and the wind. I looked outside and saw a shadow—the figure of someone who moved, an indefinite shape, a prowler whose dark form slunk toward me menacingly. Panicky, I reached for the telephone, to call the friend who lived nearby (my best, last, dearest friend; nightmares deal in superlatives and magnitudes); *he,* somehow, I knew, was the only one dear enough, close enough, to help me. But there was no answer to all my frantic ringing. Then, putting the phone down, I heard a *tap-tap-tap*ping at the window and turned to see—bared with the malignity of a fiend behind the streaming glass—the baleful, murderous face of that selfsame friend . . ."

All of us know this dream, waking or sleeping, in one or another form. Later in the same novel, the central character, Cass Kinsolving, describes another nightmare of treachery and betrayal. In the dream Cass is sent to the penitentiary. He does not know why. His uncle drives him to the gate, promising that he will have him out in a matter of hours. He knows the governor. "Yet as my uncle stopped," says Cass, "and let me out at the gate and said good-by, and as I walked through the gate and heard it clang behind me, I knew that my uncle had already either betrayed or forgotten me. . . ."

* Random House, New York, 1959. Selections from pages 5–6, 273, 274 used by permission.

In the same dream Cass is led to the gas chamber to be executed, "with the warden at my side," he says, "and two frock-coated preachers fore and aft." "And so then I woke up beneath the blanket half-smothered and howling bloody murder with the vision in my brain of the dream's last Christawful horror: which was my uncle, my kindly good old bald-headed uncle who'd reared me like a daddy, standing with a crucible of cyanide at the chamber door, grinning . . . in his round tight-fitting executioner's shroud . . ."

Treachery and betrayal. It's an old theme, older than history but as new as every new day! It has in recent years become a favorite theme of novelists, dramatists, artists, some philosophers and even theologians. In one form of existentialism the theme of betrayal embraces all of existence—total human existence becomes itself a kind of bitter, colossal betrayal of man. And this view finds eloquent expression in the plays of Tennessee Williams, for example, or Beckett's *Waiting for Godot,* or Sartre's *No Exit;* or in the compounded frustrations in Faulkner; or some of the paintings of a Soutine or a Picasso—betrayal and meaninglessness, summed up bitterly in James Gould Cozzens' phrase (in his novel, *By Love Possessed*), "the dreadful, eyeless face of existence."

In the biblical faith, of course, and in subsequent Judaism and Christianity, this bleak view of existence is vehemently denied. All the more remarkable, then, is the fact that biblical tradition and history reflect so consistently the quality of treachery. Human betrayal in one form or another is almost thematic, appearing prominently in most of the Bible's most prominent men. In the moralistic sense of the word, there are very few "good" men here. You will recall that even Jesus rejected, and with some fervor, the appellation "good." "Why do you call me good? No one is good but God alone!" (Mark 10:18 and Luke 18:19; *cf.* Matt. 19:17) The three disciples closest to Jesus once slept when asked to stand guard, and one of these, the renowned Peter, committed the treachery of denial three times in quick succession. If Judas' heinous act is quite beyond the pale, we recall that *all* the disciples deserted and so betrayed their leader in his most critical hours.

Consider David and Uriah. David is the Old Testament's king *par excellence*. Where will you find an act of human betrayal of such enormity, recounted with such undeviating faithfulness? His son, the fabulous Solomon, betrayed his father and his father's friends and, in the judgment of most historians, his own people. Solomon betrayed them all to his own pride and arrogance. This remarkable biblical honesty and realism extends even to the stories of the patriarchs. Abraham and Isaac betray their wives in the interests of their own welfare. And Jacob manages in the course of a career distinguished in treachery to deceive his dying father, rob his twin brother of his dearest possession and his father-in-law of all his portable wealth. This last series of episodes in which Jacob acquires the considerable holding of Laban produces the Bible's greatest masterpiece of understatement. With Jacob having successfully fleeced Laban of all that he has, the biblical narrative reads, "Now Jacob saw that Laban did not regard him with favor as before."

The point of all this is not for a moment to say that man in the Bible is any worse than man in any other time or place. Nor would I contend that biblical man is any better, or perhaps I may say any "gooder." Man is man, persistently producing relationships of rupture and alienation. In any time and every place sons and daughters betray parents, spouse betrays spouse, neighbor betrays neighbor, nation betrays nation, color betrays color. Who here has not himself been hurt by betrayal?

But who here can say that he has never inflicted hurt by his own act of betrayal? All of us are even now involved in the long-lived and still sustained betrayal of the American Negro, south *and* north, east and west. We have put him and other minority groups in the role of Laban or Uriah, or the Suffering Servant or the crucified Christ.

Treachery and betrayal are real enough—and it isn't any wonder that the optimism of the nineteenth century has given way in the twentieth to this kind of voguish, popular, sophisticated existential despair. And I'm quite sure, myself, that this mood of despair has been helped along not only because it has been so brilliantly articulated but because two of the most popular alternatives are so thin and false. I refer —and I'm not talking altogether in fun—to the squeaky, unrealistic good cheer of the *Reader's Digest* variety; and the pseudopsychological, pseudoreligious line of the positive thinkers.

The question is not whether man is prone to treachery and betrayal but whether in consequence or in addition existence itself is necessarily and irremediably grim and eyeless, bleak and unresponsive, meaningless and void. The question is whether and how treachery, evil, negation may be continued in an existence that is responsive and meaningful.

At lunch not long ago, in the midst of the most casual conversation, a friend and colleague in psychology asked with some apparent feeling, "What has happened in this student generation to the attributes of hope and expectation, of confidence and gratification?" From his point of view, too, it appears that we have acquiesced too much in the sense of the depressing and the tragic, the counsel of the meaningless and the unfulfilled.

Now, against the proposition of *existence* itself as betrayal, let me call in some nontheological if not antitheological support. As a believing man, let me say emphatically that if I must choose between secular apostles of existential redemption and nihilists of any stripe, give me, please, the man who believes in something. So here is Archibald MacLeish in the play *JB*. I'm about to commend the play but absolutely not for the alleged kinship of the character JB with the Old Testament Job. The biblical Job is represented by the modern JB with approximately the same fidelity that Joan of Arc can be represented by Little Orphan Annie. But if we will let JB represent JB; if in this starkly post-Christian age one simply cannot in conscience affirm faith in the Judaeo-Christian God; then by all means with JB and MacLeish let us create God by blowing on the coals of the heart, by re-creating and sustaining love in what has become a near loveless world. I've come to be grateful for my secular friends and colleagues who cannot join me in this confession but who know what it is to trust, to be gentle, to love, to forgive. And here is Thornton Wilder in *Skin of our Teeth,* with old Sabina coming in again after treachery and betrayal have done their worst, and picking up existence once more with courage and humor and vast human affection. Here, too, is William Inge, who knows that the Dark at the Top of the Stairs is dissipated by trust and acceptance and who may even suspect that the ultimate dark at the top of the bottom of existence is ultimately tolerable and penetrable. Here is James Agee in the Pulitzer Prize novel, *Death in the Family;* and here is Tad Mosel capturing that same courage and affirmation in the play from the novel—the play called *All the Way Home.* Here, in both novel and play, we are witnesses to, and participants in, a kind of secular redemption of death, the frustration of existence's ultimate betrayal.

The Bible, of course, offers what is at once an easier and infinitely more difficult ground for faith that betrayal is not the last word and that existence may be affirmative, meaningful, and joyful. What distinguishes biblical man from other men is not his goodness but his dogged, persistent confidence, in the face of all sorts of denial, that God is involved in this incredible, crazy human venture and that his impingement on existence remains itself the guarantee of the ultimate worth and meaning of existence.

Years ago Harry Emerson Fosdick wrote a sermon that has become a classic. It was entitled "A Great Time to Be Alive." I would like respectfully to insist that it is also now a great time to be alive. (We will dispense with the urgent, heroic strains in the background of the *William Tell Overture.*) It is a great time to be alive precisely because it is such a helluva time to be alive, such a frail, frangible time to be alive, such a tenuous kind of time which may not even endure as we have known it. I call you to believe in this time and this existence. I insist that if you will not believe, neither you nor I nor any of us will be established. I call you to set trust over against treachery, and gentleness and forgiveness and understanding over against all sorts of betrayal. I call you, in this trust, to leave all the broken devices of the past and come toward a land or toward the creation of a land that is, in whatever sense you must say this, God's land, the land that He will show you. I call you to nothing less than the service of the kingdom of God—under any vocabulary-service on behalf of a new land, a new world, a refreshed and re-created existence. If you will believe, you shall surely be established!

O LORD, our Lord, how excellent is thy name in all the earth. If we ask of thee, What are *we,* and What is our life, do thou help us to affirm, in such several ways as we are able, that thou art mindful of us, and that thou dost visit us. And since now, O Lord, it is of thy mercy that another day is added to our lives, do thou, we beseech thee, grant that as we grow in age we may grow in the knowledge of thy love made known in priest and prophet of old, and in Jesus Christ, our Lord. AMEN.

The Garden of Eden and The Garden of Gethsemane

by Daniel T. Niles *

(Scripture: Gen. 3:6–9)

The tree was good for food, it was pleasant to the eyes, and
it was a tree to be desired to make one wise. So they took
the fruit thereof and did eat. And their eyes were opened.
And they heard the voice of the Lord God walking in the
garden, and they hid themselves from His presence. And
the Lord God called unto Adam, and said unto him, "Where
art thou?"

Adam is on his way away from home. The days of in-
nocence are over. Paradise is left behind. He is beginning
his journey to the land of the knowledge of good and evil.
Henceforth he is free from God.

It is in the university that the student first finds how

---

* Daniel T. Niles is Principal of the Y.M.C.A. college in Ceylon and
a long-time leader in ecumenical affairs. This sermon was preached during the Third Assembly of the World Council of Churches at New Delhi.

important his own thoughts are. He has to live by them. He determines for himself what is good and what is evil, and that which he decides he has to be.

No more is there anyone to protect him from himself. In paradise his freedom was ensured by the limited authority and power which his own decisions had. Now there are no limits. He is at the mercy of his own will.

Soon enough he attaches himself to some group or groups. He must escape from the awful power of his aloneness and find protection in the codes of behavior and patterns of thought of those to whom he makes himself belong.

But that is only temporary respite, for God has refused to allow himself to be left behind. The sadness of that voice which said: "Adam, where art thou?" follows him; and from that voice there is no escaping even in the university.

The Lamb was slain from the foundations of the world. God accompanied man out of paradise. Having rebelled against being bound by God's command, he has now to live in constant flight from God's pursuit.

God is the inevitable boundary of man's life. We are either prisoners of His word or fugitives from His love.

For Christ Jesus, though He was God, counted it not something to be grasped at to cling to this glory, but emptied himself and became man and was found in the haunts of men. (See Phil. 2:6–7).

How empty Jesus was, so empty that no one feared to come to Him, and no one had any excuse for avoiding Him.

The unclean leper, even from whose shadow men shrank,

came to Jesus and Jesus touched him: an action which made Jesus himself unclean, so that for the stipulated period He could not enter any city.

Children were brought to Him when He was very tired, but He received them and took them in His arms and blessed them. The kingdom of God belonged to children, and tiredness was no reason to send them away.

An adulteress was dragged before Him. He kept His eyes averted from her lest her shame erect a barrier between Him and her: and, when she was left alone with Him, He found a way of conveying forgiveness to her.

A pharisee invited Him to dinner, but refused to treat Him as an honored guest. There was no water for His feet, nor oil for His head, nor was He given the kiss of welcome. But Jesus stayed; and at dinner that night, because of the emptiness of the Christ, God found a way of reaching Simon's soul.

"He emptied himself." That is the good news of the Christian faith. Only a stable was available, but He came. How else could we have met Him at this General Committee except that He was willing to be among us and with us whatever the conditions.

But precisely in this emptiness consists also the awkwardness of Jesus. Because of it, we are unable to keep Him away from our lives. We satisfy ourselves by offering Him a stable, and hope that He will not come to be a permanent guest: but He comes. In our work, in our thoughts, in our plans, even in our prayers, there is only a stable for Him, and yet He is there.

The Student Christian Movement is set in the university to be a common stable where the Christ will come: and, because the Christ comes, there is also in the university an echo of those words spoken to Adam: "Adam, where art thou?"

The Lamb was slain from the foundations of the world. God accompanied man out of paradise. So that even the student in the university must come to terms with Him. What shall he do?

Each student takes his own road, but ultimately all roads lead to Gethsemane. It is to Gethsemane that the road from Bethlehem leads, the road by which Jesus comes; it is also to Gethsemane that the road from paradise leads, the road by which Judas arrives. So that, here in Gethsemane, God and man meet again.

"Adam, where art thou?"—that is how the story began; "Friend, why are you here?"—that is how the story comes to its climax.

"Jesus came to the disciples and said to them, Are you still sleeping? Behold the hour is at hand and my betrayer is near. Then came Judas, and with him a great crowd with swords and clubs, and he came up to Jesus and kissed Him. Jesus said to him, 'Friend, why are you here?'" (See Matt. 26:45–50.)

Judas had committed his life to a cause which was the cause of his people. God would restore the kingdom to Israel, and God's Messiah would come. So that, in accepting to follow Jesus, Judas accepted Him as the answer to all his plans and all his hopes. Here was a discipleship which commanded all that he had to give.

But Jesus had broken loose from the plans that Judas had made for Him. God had wriggled away from under. And the freedom which Judas had found for himself, which was built on imprisoning God, now lay shattered because Jesus had His own way which He would take.

Jesus comes even if it be a stable we have to offer, but we cannot make Him at home there. It is our stable until He comes, but once He comes it is His territory, the spearhead of His thrust into the whole area of our lives, the bridgehead from which He will move into full occupation. No wonder that we seek the only way out which is possible, which is to betray Him.

Have you been to Gethsemane? Do you know what it means to betray the Son of Man as your last desperate effort to make Him serve your ends? Do your lips tremble at the remembrance of that kiss which you gave Him when you sought to deliver Him over to His enemies in order that you may keep Him for yourself?

Or is it your situation that you have not yet arrived at Gethsemane, that you still find it possible to support the company of Jesus without feeling any radical opposition to Him and without encountering any radical opposition between His plans and your own?

Only those who have stood face to face with Jesus at Gethsemane know the devastating power of the words with which He greeted them: "Friend, why are you here?"—and the overwhelming humility with which He allowed them to take him captive. He emptied himself, and being found in human form He humbled himself and became obedient unto death.

How often we have seen this event take place in the university, in the S.C.M., in the lives of individual students: God at man's mercy because God will not leave man alone even on his journey away from paradise; and man, therefore, seeking ways of rejecting God, of ejecting Him!

It is in Gethsemane that we discover that we are rebels; and that discovery we must make. Someday each one of us must see, if we have not already so seen, how brittle is our moral nature, how deceitful are our intellectual processes, and how possessive is even the very dedication by which we live. And this vision will not come until we ourselves, as Judas did, stand afar off and watch Him die whom we had betrayed.

He emptied himself, He became ours. He humbled himself, He put himself at our mercy. He was obedient unto death, He accepted the fate we had decreed for Him. Is it any wonder that He calls himself our servant and demands that we accept His service if we wish to have anything to do with Him at all? It is easy to call Him Lord, it is difficult to accept Him as servant.

That night when He washed the feet of the disciples, Simon Peter would not allow Him to wash his feet. Jesus said to him, "Simon, if I do not wash you, you have no part in me." You must accept the service I have come to bring. "For the Son of Man came not to be ministered unto but to minister and to give His life a ransom for many."

The Hindu finds it easy to speak of Jesus as God incarnate, but he will not accept Him as Saviour. The Buddhist is willing to speak of the Lord Jesus, but he will not accept His grace. The Muslim is willing to speak of Isa Nabi, but he will not accept His forgiveness.

Authority can take many forms. A mother's authority over her child is the authority of one who serves. So was the authority of Jesus. It took the form of a servant. We need to be broken by the humility of Jesus before we can realize who He is and what it is that He wants from us.

Is Jesus your servant? Has He done for you what you could not do for yourself? Is He doing for you what you cannot do for yourself? To ask the age-old question: Are you washed in the blood of the Lamb?

I looked, and behold, a great multitude, which no man could number, from every nation, from all tribes and peoples and tongues . . . clothed in white robes, with palm branches in their hands, and crying out with a loud voice, "Salvation belongs to our God . . . and to the Lamb."
"Who are these, clothed in white robes? . . . These are they who . . . have washed their robes and made them white in the blood of the Lamb. Therefore are they before the throne of God, and serve Him day and night . . ." (Rev. 7:9–15)

Thus do men go forward on their journey: from paradise through the dusty roads of Galilee to Gethsemane, and from Gethsemane along the *via dolorosa* to Calvary, and from Calvary—where?

Judas went and bought the potter's field and hanged himself. He could not bear any longer the love of Jesus Christ. But oh, how wasteful that was—wasteful of his life, wasteful of his repentance, wasteful of God's forgiving grace! Judas could not forget himself even in his repentance. Even in his repentance, he had to be master of his own life.

We do not truly repent until we have received that repentance itself as a gift from our Lord, as part of His service to us; and so find ourselves delivered finally from being at the mercy of our own will. . . . And then?

And then, along the paths of our obedience as well as our disobedience, we meet Him, the Lord of our lives as He is the Lord of life, whose will for us has become again the acknowledged boundary of our existence; and we find paradise again in the mastery of His fellowship.

Saul was on his way to Damascus; Jesus met him along the way. So to us, too, it will happen that He will meet us on every Damascus road, waylaying us along life's journey when we take the wrong turning, even sending us blindness with respect to those things which He will not have us undertake, and asking us to go to the house which He has prepared for us where it shall be told us what we must do.

"Within the fellowship of the Church"—there our journey ends: and begins.

BLESSED BE the God and Father of our Lord Jesus Christ, who through Jesus Christ destined us in love to be His sons according to the purpose of His will; and sealed us with the Holy Spirit the guarantee of our inheritance; to the praise of His glorious grace which He freely bestowed on us in the Beloved. AMEN. (See Eph. 1:3–14.)

Lidice and Coventry

by Francis B. Sayre, Jr.*

(Scripture: "And behold, there arose a great storm on
the sea: . . . but he was asleep. And they went and woke
him, saying, 'Save, Lord; we are perishing.' And he said
to them: 'Why are you afraid, O men of little faith?'
Then he rose and rebuked the winds and the sea; and
there was a great calm." Matt. 8:24–26)

Surely a storm at sea is a terrifying thing! I was once on a
ship that was all but broken in two by a hurricane. She held
together only by a few twisted plates of steel. Like the disciples, in their little boat, the crew and I commended ourselves to God's mercy; and I suppose that our fear betrayed
our little faith. But such a tempest, upon the waters of the
deep, is but a tiny squall compared to the holocausts that
sweep through history—the wars and empires, revolution
and slaughter. We, who live at this moment in the after-
math of the most devastating of these turmoils, are aware
that the vessel of man's common life is sundered all but in
twain. It hangs together by a few twisted strands: a world

* Francis B. Sayre, Jr. is Dean of the Washington Cathedral.

58

divided and broken, in danger of the final break which will send it to the depths.

Those who had known Christ, by that Sea of Galilee, remembered Him later on when the wrath of the Roman Empire crackled about their ears. They remembered how He alone stilled the storm and gave calm. They recorded in their Bibles the story of the lake, knowing now that it was the truth of all history. Through Christ's love the holocaust is quelled and brokenness healed.

There are some in the world today who believe this. But many more do not. Never was the watershed between them of little faith and them of none made plainer to me than by two visits—in the space of six days last week—to two towns newly rebuilt after their destruction by the Nazis.

The first of these was Lidice, that quiet village in Czechoslovakia of which the Germans made a dreadful example by killing every male inhabitant, imprisoning the women and children, and flattening every house literally to the ground. But it was no joy to see the new village erected by the Communist regime of the latter day. For hate had been answered by hate. We were taken to no homes of Christian folk, but only to see the gruesome film the Germans themselves had taken of the slaughter. We were shown the museum where the pitiful remains are preserved; the monument that records in granite every other atrocious obliteration of hapless cities wiped out by war. Most of all we missed the lovely church, which had stood at the center of old Lidice. There was no church at all in the new town; only hate and fear— fear of Germany and hatred of the West for contributing to

German rearmament. It seemed as if amid the vivid memory of the bitter storm, Christ alone had been forgotten.

The other town was Coventry in England: victim of the same Nazi ferocity; now built up again with great good sense in modern dress—and all on a human scale, rather than with the madness that defiles our American cities by deifying the motorized wheel. People count in England, and the chief street in the new Coventry is a mall for pedestrians only. But the heart of Coventry is still the cathedral, built anew in modern idiom, perfectly related to the humane concept of all else in the new-sprung city.

In the forecourt of the new cathedral is the shrine that contrasts so poignantly with Lidice. The forecourt of the new is the nave of the old cathedral, now planted in grass, still outlined by the broken tracery of its charred windows. There, where the high altar once stood, stones are piled, crowned by a cross made of two ancient spikes from the roof. And behind this cross are written just the two words: *"Father Forgive."* When one stands in that place, the holy whisper of Christ is almost audible, as He rebukes the wind and the sea. And the people of Coventry, forgiving, in imitation of Him, have received sixteen boys and girls from Germany who have given a year of their labor to help rebuild this shrine of peace. They gave me tea, there among the ruins.

Lidice—and Coventry! Hate and healing! Fear of the storm—and the shelter of faith! At first I thought that these were symbols of East and West: signs of a differing temper on either side of the Iron Curtain. It is perhaps understandable that we Americans should be caught prisoner by our own propaganda and come to believe that everything on the other side is atheism, while God can only rejoice in the temperateness of our own culture on the hither side. However, my recent sojourn in Czechoslovakia illumined for me the fact that faith dwells on both sides of the political boundary. The truth is that "In Christ there is no East or West."

Five days spent in conference with Christian leaders of Russia, Poland, Hungary, Czechslovakia, and Eastern Germany—and two more days preaching and visiting in two parish churches in Prague—confirmed the holy communion which no political or military force can breach. Christianity in the Russian orbit has been stripped of any complacency, any advantage, any security it may once have had. There it costs dear to confess the faith. A pastor's child may not enter a university but is condemned by the father's profession to a life of manual labor. Those who openly attend Divine Worship are the last to be promoted to any job worth having. Yet I preached, unannounced by any advance notice, to congregations well populated by young and old—even soldiers in uniform who dared to go. All received me with love, the kind of love that prompted an old man to press an apple into my hand after service—precious gift for him! The kind of love that yearned for communication and understanding across the world's dread barricades, knowing that Christ alone can calm the storm and redeem the time.

Nor did our brothers behind the Iron Curtain allow their

American visitors to think of them as pitiable remnants of some little engulfed coterie. Rather they presented themselves as a little band of disciples on the march, not defending, but attacking—out to conquer, by the Holy Spirit, the whole man-centered crass ideology of the Marxist masters, just as centuries ago the Twelve pitted themselves against the Empire of Rome. Stripped of all fat, shorn of the comfortable irrelevance of the past, these men and women are seeking to come to terms in their lives with whatever is good in the economic revolution with which, for better or worse, they have to live; but at the same time to wrestle with the terrible emptiness, the soul-killing futility, of the Communist doctrine.

When I prayed with them, when together we said the Litany from our own prayer book, I thought of that story of Joshua which was read this morning: how Moses sent him forth to spy out the land of Canaan which God had promised; how he came back to report that it was a goodly land, but that it was peopled with a race of giants, who looked upon Joshua and Caleb as no more than grasshoppers. "The land we have explored is a land that eateth up its inhabitants." Such is a Communist country today. "Nevertheless," said Joshua, "the Lord has given us this good land!" And such is the spirit of Christians behind the Iron Curtain at this moment!

No, Lidice is not the sign of all that is behind the Iron Curtain, for there is love beside the hatred, in the courage of our Christian brothers who brave the storm in the strength of Christ. It is good, surely, that we can be in touch with them—and with them pray that somehow, perhaps beyond comprehension, the Son of Man shall bring calm to the tossing tempest of our life.

There is one thing more. I would not leave the impression with you that such a prayer is the final culmination of Christian communion. If all we can finally do together is only to echo the disciples in their plea, "Save, Lord, we perish," then surely Christ must turn to us with the same words of old, "Why are ye fearful, O ye of little faith?" Nor did the recent colloquy of Christian from East and West in fact end there. Whereas we began by discussing our differences—exploring the divergent contexts of our situations, trying to see in each other's reflection the delicate line that separates all of our compromises from our principle—we came gradually to realize that despite the divergent setting on either side of the Iron Curtain, we are all confronted by basically the same challenge. And that is the challenge of a brand now age: an age of exploding knowledge and immense technical possibility; an age industrialized and secularized, which on both sides of the Curtain is absorbed with man and his infinite potentiality, his incorrigible sin, but which no longer speaks the language or thinks the thoughts of God.

In Coventry there is still forgiveness, but still Coventry is really no more the salient symbol of the West than is Lidice of the East. For all of us in common are engulfed in a moment of history, poised upon the threshold of space, that has reshuffled every familiar landmark of earth, requiring of us immeasurably deeper knowledge of creation and radically new categories of understanding the saving grace of God in Jesus Christ.

We came to see that in many ways we Christians resemble Christopher Columbus, who thought he would reach familiar Cathay by sailing westward, but who in reality came upon a brand-new world. When he got there, nothing fitted the frame of his expectation. All geography had to be revised. It may well be true that Christians the world over are in that situation. Reality is no longer described by the old categories, theological and ecclesiastical, by which in centuries past we tried to comprehend the mystery of God at the center of all things. Before the mystery of this truth, the differences of East and West pale to inconsequentiality —as did the fears of the disciples at Galilee. And by the same token, the healing wonder of God's victory in Christ is greatly magnified, and captures our lives anew in the blessedness of the calm beyond the storm. God grant that in the age at hand we may together come to a new understanding of that holy peace.

The Church Under The Cross

by Reinold von Thadden-Trieglaff*

(Scripture: "The word of the Cross is folly to those that
are perishing, but to us who are being saved it is the
power of God." I Cor. 1:18)

"Church under the cross!" Dear friends, does not this theme
appear old-fashioned to millions of people in our time? During my imprisonment in Russia twelve years ago and, later,
in that period of my life when I visited German prisoners
of war in Belgium, France, Italy, Egypt and North Africa,
the strong impression grew on me that this is really the
situation. It was my opportunity to talk to large numbers
of comrades who adhered to very different philosophies of
life and who had widely divergent political and religious
views. And I was constantly asked what the church actually

* Reinold von Thadden-Trieglaff is President of the *Deutscher Evan-
gelischer Kirchentag* and a long-time leader in ecumenical affairs. This
sermon was preached at the Lutheran World Assembly in Minneapolis,
1957.

means in proclaiming the cross of Jesus Christ and placing it on altars and graves. When in later years I began to work for the German Evangelical *Kirchentag,* I again received many letters and held conversations with many visitors which pointed in the same direction. I believe we do well to face these questions, because they illuminate the situation in which we find ourselves.

To begin with, we must take into account one strong suspicion on the part of our contemporaries, which can be condensed into the sentence: Is not the church under the cross really the *church in retreat?* And does not this impression seem primarily the result of developments in the postwar years? We have seen countless people turn to the church after the war, with open hearts and great hope. We witnessed their earnestness and the confidence which made them expect something good from the church. And we now see the disappoinment with which these people turn away again from the church. "We came, but the church was not there," they say. "The church we met was not the church we were looking for. It was the church of the past, the church of restoration, the church in complete retreat from the real battlefields of our time."

The second accusation which we hear concentrates in this reproach: The church under the cross is a church which is always indulging in thoughts about itself. What can we make of a church that wastes its precious time striving for bolstering up of its dogma? How often in history, when weighty tasks were at stake in the world, has it seemed as if the church used the largest part of its strength to mediate about itself! It met the most burning issues either with a "correct" theology, or with a retreat into its own self-sufficiency.

The third reproach is: the church under the cross is a *mere ideal*. When the church starts to talk about it, it takes refuge in an imaginary dream which it will never be able to realize. We know these pictures which the church draws of its own life, when it describes how things should be. In reality, facts are quite different, people justly say. Everybody can see that the church suffers from the same diseases that trouble all the world. When, because of nervous activity in the world, one finds no time for reflection and rest, it is just the same in the church. When one is worn out by the dissensions in the world, the dissensions in the church seem almost more severe and are fought out with even greater rancor. The church which pretends to be a church under the cross, only wishes to escape its own reality. At the same time, it is a church that cannot even help itself, let alone help others.

It cannot be denied, dear friends, that with this reproach we are getting to the root of the *meaning of the cross of Jesus Christ*. For this very reason, however, let me first agree that all these reproaches are justified to a certain extent. The church itself has furnished much material for these misunderstandings and accusations. Nevertheless, I believe that the theme "church under the cross" is of paramount interest for us. Therefore I shall try and explain what the cross of Jesus Christ means to me, and what I imagine to be a true "church under the cross" today.

What actually does the cross represent? It is the place where it becomes manifest what God did in identifying His Son, and thereby Himself, with the rebellious and godless world. It is the place where God proved once and for all that He loves man for His own sake. It is the place where God sealed with His blood the assurance that, in spite of everything, He has not written off and forsaken man, but meets him amidst the terrible realities of life, exactly at the point of his sin, his fear and torment, exactly there. . . . That is the whole Gospel.

These profound perspectives of the cross illuminate the church in its very essence. They condemn the church where it wants to be more than Christ, where it wants to live more easily and less painfully than He. At the same time, the Cross of Jesus Christ who triumphed over death on Easter Morning, paves the way to the tasks of the Church, the proclamation of the Gospel and the service of its fellow-men.

What we say of the Cross concerns first the *form* of the Church, secondly its *life* and thirdly its *mission*.

A Church under the Cross cannot present itself other than in the "form of a servant." It must always remember that its Lord and Master was at all times and under all circumstances concerned for the poor, the miserable and the sick. It must never give occasion for the reproach that it has a secret tendency to side with the privileged classes and professions, and of itself striving for greater honour and esteem in this world. When our Lord Jesus Christ saw the multitudes which had gathered round Him, He "was moved with compassion on them, for they were as sheep without a shepherd."

But the Church often enough thinks only of its own sheep at this moment, although it is the task of the Church under the Cross to meet in genuine *solidarity* all those who have lost their way in the maze of this world. Today, the manifold problems of many groups are at stake. There is the host of refugees, of expellees and uprooted people all over the world. There are the misled, who have been given deceitful promises by false prophets and who, before long, will face new disillusionment. There are those whose personal life has been caught in the pitiless machinery of the frightening tensions of the world, and who do not understand why they of all people should be the victims of these tensions. All these people should find a home in the Church under the Cross which, according to its New Testament character, declares its solidarity with them all.

The church under the cross is also a church of *brotherhood*. In the New Testament we read that the disciples first fled from the cross and then scattered. But then, after Whitsuntide, the cross became the great sign of their fellowship under which they gathered for worship and for the Lord's Supper. Suddenly, the original symbol of disgrace and weakness became for the early church the symbol of service, a beacon of helpful and unselfish love, the center of a community that was prepared to bear witness and to suffer. This does not belong only to past days; we can also experience it today. It has happened, for instance, at the assemblies of the German Evangelical *Kirchentag* since 1949. When in Leipzig, in the Soviet-controlled East Zone, 650,000 people flocked together in a wide park under a huge cross, the impossible came true: this enormous crowd of poor and desperately lonely individuals grew into a community, a fellowship of faith, a fellowship of love. And when the hundreds of thousands returned home, they went back into their old distressing conditions of living with courage and confidence.

When we read today the biblical accounts of the "likemindedness" of the first Christians, we read them wrongly if we only admire them from a distance, while contenting ourselves with the assumption that this is not again possible until the return of our Lord Jesus Christ at the end of all things. As if the apostles' exhortations to likemindedness and brotherly readiness to help were mere pious verbalizations! I believe that today more than ever it is insufferable when a church under the cross harbors in its own ranks problems of personal prestige, when parties are formed around individual men to fight one another, when the leaders speak and act according to mere tactical points of view, or when those who who should be advocates of a great cause struggle ruthlessly for power and prominence.

It is impossible to exaggerate how much a church in which fraternal likemindedness is practiced and lived means for the world. We experience in our days tensions that can scarcely be resolved. The democratic and parliamentary rules, which originally came from the spirit of Christian fellowship, lost this background long ago, even in the Western countries, and often prove to be incapable of easing disputes. In the end, the drive for self-assertion seems to be victorious. Therefore a church desiring to be a church under the cross can contemplate its own dividedness and dissensions only with much sorrow. It cannot rest satisfied with the knowledge that, at this point, too, it shares the fate of the whole world. It must rather prove capable of overcoming its tensions and of practicing fraternal likemindedness. The cross is not the sign of divergence, but of community.

That the church stands under the cross of Jesus Christ has also its effects on the *life of the church*. In this connection I wish to refer to two points:

A church under the cross is an *obedient* church, since its Master was the One who "became obedient unto death, even death on a cross" (Phil. 2:8). This is the particular secret of His sonship and His freedom. We see Him speak and act in incredible freedom. He is in a position to disregard all limitations, even those considered permanent and immovable. It is nothing for Him to attack and to break through holy traditions. He mixes with people of bad reputation. He undertakes to give a new interpretation of the will of God. Finally, He even runs the risk that powerful and influential men will rise up against Him in a united front. He preserves His freedom and independence in every direction. He can do all this only because of His complete obedience to God.

The church under the cross attests with its life: Only he who obeys God is truly free. Thereby the church gives up all calculation. It will keep silent where it has no mission. It will speak when ordered by God, even when it seems inopportune. It is allowed to choose neither the subjects of its speeches nor its fields of action. It finds itself faced with given themes and is directed to particular men and groups of men. Exactly in such obedience the church shows what distinctive freedom it has been granted. It can tackle its tasks wherever they are set before it, without paying heed to the question whether, by the human measure, they are feasible or not. It can change the fronts of action as often as it is impelled to, without having to pay attention to charges of inconsistency. It can do all this if it is an obedient church.

In the end, such a church will also be a *suffering* church; it cannot be otherwise. Whoever tries to be completely obedient to God in this world will soon learn what the world thinks about that. This is true even where the church is still considered useful by the worldly rulers. Even if the church is in a position to furnish many positive contributions to fulfil the plans of the governors in the worldly sphere, it carries a message that is never convenient: Repent and be converted! Carrying the great warning, the church will always remain inconvenient. It will help to realize what is possible and attainable at the moment; it will rejoice at every step forward in dealing with the world's problems. But simultaneously it will always strive beyond this and seek to start the healing process at the actual seat of the disorder. It will be obliged to hurt men as well as nations, when it brings down all kinds of self-righteousness. Therefore the church has little prospect of popularity.

This particularly holds true when enmity prevails against its Master, Jesus Christ. Then it becomes most clearly evident that the church under the cross is a suffering church. We all know that the churches in the Russian sphere of influence are suffering churches. Also, the church in East Germany is being led into suffering. But we are greatly mis-

taken if we believe that at such points the church is deprived
of all power, that it cannot do anything but passively bear
every blow which the malice and wantonness of the powerful may devise. This is not the case for the very reason that
the church under the cross seeks to take upon itself its sufferings just as its Master took upon Himself His sufferings.
Thereby the initiative lies with the church itself. It is the
great secret of the cross and of suffering under the cross
that it does not mean the end and does not lead to surrender;
it is the purpose for which the Son of the Lord came down
to earth and brought the beginning of a new life. Therefore
we have to maintain the connection with our suffering
brother-churches by all possible means: they guard for us
the most precious treasure that has been given to the church
for its life.

That the church stands under the cross of Jesus Christ
is, finally, meaningful for the *mission of the church*. Again
I should like to stress two points:

A church under the cross is a *vicarious* church. What
Jesus Christ accomplished on His way to the cross was vicarious action. He made the situation of the world His own.
To a church that looks to the cross, awareness of the needs
of the world will not be hindered; rather the church will be
enabled to see the world as it is and to enter into its intense
needs. And the serious question arises for all of us, ourselves
and our churches: When and where have we made the situation of men and nations our own? The world will not bring
its needs and perplexities before God. It revolts or despairs,
it rages or resigns. We, however, can take its fate upon our

shoulders and vicariously bring it before God. What other use should the church make of its knowledge of the remission of sins? It knows indeed better than the world what unforgiven guilt means. It knows better how unforgiven guilt separates, for instance, the nations and prevents peace. What use does the church make of the intercession entrusted to it? The world is waiting for the vicarious service of a church under the cross.

In the light of all this, a further point should be clear. A church under the cross is the exact opposite of an introverted and contemplative company. It is a *church for the world*. This insight has been given us during the past fifteen years. As yet it seems as if the church with all its mobility and inventive impulsiveness, with all its alertness and persistence, has had only one aim, namely to be counted among the acknowledged powers of this world—at least as an equally acknowledged partner. It still has to disprove this impression. It must become manifest that the church exists *for* the world and *in* the world, but is *not like* the world. A church under the cross is the loyal protector who ventures into the dangerpoints of the world's affairs, which does not shrink from touching hot iron, which is on the spot with its warning before the switches on the track are moved in the wrong direction. The church can never be an easy partner who is ready to conform. Its Lord and Master has given unchanging form to the way of salvation. So it can be a church for the world only as a church under the cross.

We can say all this solely because we know that Good Friday is followed by the Easter morning of Resurrection.

Therefore we know too that the cross is the sign of our Lord's victory. The risen Lord has not changed His identity. He still rules the whole world as the crucified Lord. He still gathers His church under His cross. Thus the church is placed in the midst of our age. What does the world *expect* from it? Perhaps very little. But what does the world *need*? It certainly needs people with new ideas, but—much more —people with a living faith. It certainly needs people who speculate upon new ways, but—much more—people who are prepared to follow Christ on His way. It certainly does not need merely interested camp-followers, but disciples who display the close connection of their lives with the cross of Jesus Christ. The world needs a church under the cross!

True Freedom

by Helmut Gollwitzer *

(Scripture: "For freedom Christ has set us free; stand fast
therefore . . ." Gal. 5:1a)

This text is given us as a motto for the whole year just
begun: 1958. Every day of this year is to stand under the
sign of this text. Every day, however it may be, sunny or
cloudy, it will point us to blessing and responsibility, direct
us to what is vital. Every day it will open a door, even when
we think that all the doors are closed to us. If we note it
and understand it, it is the most helpful, most comforting,
and most important word that could possibly be spoken to
us. If this year we begin every day with it, then truly something will happen in our life, then something will change—
and that for the good.

The text is not easy to understand. The whole world
talks about liberty and freedom. Along with the word

---

* Helmut Gollwitzer is Professor at the Free University in Berlin. This
sermon was preached at the St. Ann's Church in Berlin-Dahlem, where
Dr. Gollwitzer was assistant to Pastor Martin Niemoeller in 1937, when
the famous resister was sent to prison.

"peace," there is scarcely a word more misused today in the East and in the West than the word "freedom." Everyone thinks he knows what freedom means. But we soon perceive that in this verse of the apostle Paul the word "liberty" has another meaning from the usual. The way in which he speaks of "liberty" is not as easy to understand as a lead article in the newspaper which deals with "freedom." What then does it mean? Must we ask Paul: "What do you mean, 'Christ has set us free'?" What has freedom to do with Christ? And how can the apostle say to the Galatians and to all of us: "You are free!"? Then it is that we notice that the text is not so simple. Freedom as something wished for, as a high ideal—that we understand, and that we applaud. But how many of us could stand up right now and declare: "*I am free,* I am a free man!"? The challenge to us to do that brings to mind all the slaveries in which we are caught. We are dependent on the benevolence of some boss or other, fastened like spokes into the mechanics of some bureau or factory. The businessman is under the lash of competition. Members of the so-called free professions are more vulnerable to the pressure of advertising needs than the civil servants and employees, among whom the lack of freedom in their work is open to the light of day. Within, we are under the rule of our drives and ambitions, our prejudices, our aversions and bitterness. Merely the anxious New Year's question, "What will this year bring us?", betrays clearly enough what unfree people we are. That is as true of the Christians as of heathen. What then is Paul trying to say?

We get a little glimpse of it when we have once experienced, or at least been told, what a person witnesses to when he says: "I am freed through Jesus Christ." Something like that is said by the one who is freed from the fears and terrors of a heathen service to idols, or by the one who has been lifted by the forgiveness of sins out of the depths of an agonizing guilt-consciousness, or by the one who has been liberated by Christ from the unbreakable chains of a vice which had enslaved him, or by the one who has been strengthened in bomb shelters or in religious persecution to pass from all fear to a free, joyful confession of faith. Such people, who draw a deep breath beside us and give testimony: "Christ made me free," give us a sign, an inkling, of what Paul had in mind. And they wake in us a longing that we might experience the same emancipation.

But how can Paul say to all of us: "The same is true for you. You can say the same. You are free!"? At the turn of the year we are made aware how every moment of our life is a step out of the past into the future. We stand on the swell of time—behind us the old year we have known, before us the utterly unknown future. We think to know where we have come from and not to know where we are going. And only at one point nothing seems changed: in this, that in the new year we shall be just as unfree as in the old. But now Paul changes the picture and says: the true past is something quite different, and the true future is something quite different. Where do you come from? You think: out of the year 1957 with its good luck and its unhappiness, in any case carrying the impressions, scars and chains of pages which are in no sense blank but rather written full—altogether, as old folks with the great burden of the past. "No," says Paul. "Things are changed. Have you forgotten Christmas again, so quickly? Don't you come out of Christmas?—Christmas, understood not as a comfortable, fleeting holiday, but as an actuality, the fact of Christ. When you now look back, you see not only your own past but another past as well. Now you have *two* pasts, and they fight against each other: each asserts a different meaning. A new past replaces the old in the words of the apostle, makes the old past truly old and past, draws a line through it and draws all attention to itself: "God was in Christ reconciling the world to himself." (II Cor. 5:19) That is where we come from. We come from Bethlehem and Golgotha. That God himself has come into our lack of freedom, "born under the law" (Gal. 4:4), that he has submitted himself to our dependencies, has taken our chains upon himself, that he himself has died our death and made our grave his grave —that is the unbelievable, divine history out of which we come, which we cannot undo, out of which we can only draw the consequences for our life. Our earlier history, our origin, our point of departure, is Christ. As the racer must have solid footing at the start of the race in order to get away fast, so Paul plants our foot on this divine history— for the whole new year, and for every day of the year. This is true: the other past is no longer yours; leave it behind. *This* past in Christ—it can and shall control your future. That is the preparation with which you can live further, in anything and regardless of what may come. If you have a difficult decision and know not what to do, then first be clear on this: Where do I come from? What is certain in any case? What is the basis from which I must think my way further? It is Christ, God acting for us, God present in our midst, the grace of God, God's purpose. Strive to carry along your bad past, and it will plague and embitter and dictate further ways of evil. Away with it! It has nothing more to say. Christ is my past: he alone is worthy! If you come into temptation, out of greediness for life or anxiousness for a bit of good fortune or from fear of men, ask this: "Who stands by me? Who has taken my side? On whom can I count?" Christ my brother, my Lord, God in our midst, to whom nothing is impossible, who is faithful and gives strengths of which we formerly had no inkling. The two pasts which fight here with each other are those of our birth and our baptism. Unfortunately it is more a beautiful saying than a reality when Schiller says, "Man is created free, is free—were he born in chains." We are born into lack of freedom, as those who are unfree. We are not guiltless little children, but burdened in our earthly measure by the whole past of the human race. We are not free: we must first become free. With baptism comes something new: liberty enters our life. In baptism there comes to us one through whose power and presence in this utterly old life something new can happen. Take your stand by baptism against birth: that means, witness to freedom against lack of it. Thus Paul draws our attention rightly to the past— and at the same time shows us what lies ahead.

He addresses us as men who stand on the swell of time,

he opens the door wide and says: "What you have behind you is Christ. And what you have before you is liberty." And it remains so throughout the whole year. Every day, in every important hour, Paul will stand beside us through this Text-of-the-Year and whisper: "Think how things are: Christ behind you, liberty before you!" What is meant here by liberty you will first know when you ask not "from what," but—first—"for what" is a man free when we say that he is "free." Naturally it is the manner and style of freedom that I should be free of everything which prevents me from doing what I wish. And to be free in this sense is indeed something quite wonderful, as some of you will have discovered when released from some prison or camp or other. All of a sudden one stands on the street; he can go where he will, mount the streetcar to go to the right or to the left without someone giving orders. This wonderful freedom from all hindrances, this being able to decide for one's self, certainly belongs to the way of freedom. We can say it more exactly: it is the form of freedom—but it is not the meaning of freedom. I have known comrades who confused the two, who in prison dreamed of nothing else but to live in freedom only for that which pleased them at the moment. In so far as they later lived at home according to this precept, they fell under the wheels and slipped into greater, deeper lack of freedom than there in Russia. *For what* are we free? That is the decisive question of our life. To what end are we freed through Christ? Through this question we come to understand the meaning of Christian liberty. To be free means to be unhindered for that which I count good. This is ex-

pressed, for instance, by a person whom we urge to be reconciled with another: "I see clearly that that would be
good, but I'm not free to do it." What do we understand
to be good? For what are we made free by Christ? In the
Epistle to the Romans Paul says that through Christ we
have "access to this grace" (Rom. 5:2), and in the Epistle
to the Hebrews it is said once that through the blood of
Christ we have the joy of entrance into the Holy. And the
word which Luther originally used in his translation in
place of "joyfulness" (*Freudigkeit*) was an old-fashioned
German word, "boldness" (*Freidigkeit*). And it says something more than joyfulness, namely a joyful openness (*Frei-
mut*) with which we run into the sanctuary of God—as
children run utterly fearlessly to the father. That then is
freedom at the summit: the liberty of a good conscience
through the forgiveness of sins, a free approach to the father,
to speak with God as beloved children with their beloved
father, permission to enter into God's presence and not to
have to fear it. All is done away with which prevented the
approach: the impurity, our stained hands and hearts, our
doubt, our lack of faith—everything that you can suggest
as a reason why you cannot and may not pray. All of that is
passed away, and a great permit is placed in your hand: you
may come to communion, to church, to the throne of God,
into heaven, into the kingdom of God. That doesn't come
of itself: for that, one certainly needs permission. In my
Bavarian homeland it is a genteel custom that a guest waits
as he enters and takes his place, until the invitation has been
given. And then to this invitation he responds, "I take the

liberty." (*"Ich bin so frei."*) Jesus is the great invitation of God to the sinners, to those who stand outside, to those who don't belong: "You may come!" And faith and prayer are nothing other than our thankful answer: "I take the liberty." Freedom is grace, and to believe is to make use of the freedom presented to us through grace.

Christ not only opened the door to God but also toward people. It is not just that our old way, because of everything which was piled up and which we had to carry with us, had blocked the door to God; so too it had closed the door toward people. When the door of paradise fell into place behind Adam and Eve, a wall came between them too. And their children, Cain and Abel, couldn't approach each other either. Think now of all the times during the last year when a door fell into place between you and other people. Think of the Iron Curtain which is drawn right down the middle of our country, which in recent weeks has been made especially thick, which surrounds us so closely here in West Berlin. Think of the fact that the two German governments do not speak to each other, and that at present the most disputed issue in world politics is whether negotiations are to take place between East and West—and whether such are meaningful or not, or whether on both sides the pressures must be intensified more and more. All of this is a sign of the worst lack of freedom: there sits each party on his own island and is in the right, and the other side is wrong, and our being in the right is the iron bar that barricades the door. This pharisaism is not lodged only among heathens and atheists, but just as much among Christians.

That happens often: piety makes us unfree, anxious in the face of science, anxious in the face of human beings—just as at the time of Jesus the pious lacked the freedom to sit with tax-gatherers and sinners at the table. Anxiety and lack of freedom belong together. We have anxiety about forgiving something, anxiety that we be outplayed by others, anxiety that we won't make out well enough, anxiety for our status and our good reputation. And therefore we are not free for one another, and each one remains sitting on his throne instead—or at the most spying with the telescope upon the other, following his movements with suspicion and constantly on the defense against him.

That is the way the person who is isolated must act—the person who must look after himself because no one else cares for him. That is the person in the stance of defensiveness. But the Christian man, coming from Bethlehem and Golgotha, is the man who no longer has to look after himself. His is not to react in an unfree way. He doesn't have to barricade himself any more. For him, the door to the neighbor has been opened. That is why a few verses later in our chapter Paul enlarges the word "freedom" with the word "love," and comments: "only do not use your freedom as an opportunity for the flesh"—in other words, use your freedom for your own egoism—"but through love be servants of one another!" Now everything is quite clear. The *form* of freedom is this: to be able to decide for one's self. The *secret* of freedom is this: to be without anxiety for one's self. And the *meaning* of freedom is this: Love. This is the exact meaning of the beautiful old saying, upon which we cannot meditate too often: *Deo servire summa libertas.* "To serve God is the highest freedom." Whenever in the coming year you find yourself in the stance of defense against your neighbor, whenever you sense a hindrance to think of your neighbor with love and charity, then recognize it as lack of freedom, as a contradiction to the freedom into which Christ has freed us. Back off from it and turn again toward freedom.

The lack of freedom of the blocked door, the pharisaical self-justification, the anxiety toward the other, rule today the whole world. And if God leaves us to our sins, then we shall all be shipwrecked by it. The world cries today for nothing so much as for Christians, who are freed from this lack of freedom, who break with abandon through all the iron curtains, who recognize even in scoundrels God's beloved creation, who first ask in every case of enmity toward Christ where our own Christian lack of freedom may bear the guilt, who seek not to defend themselves from the Communists but rather bring to the Communists God's love and freedom, who step into the cleft of the divided world and build bridges and perform the Samaritan service on all sides —without being concerned whether for it they will be misunderstood and reviled from all sides. In her history the church has been crippled again and again because she let herself be drawn inwardly into defensiveness, into self-assertion. Today, too, she is in this danger, and in many places the Christians are crippled in their service by anxiety and pharisaism. The fighting camps of the East and the West both want to put the church to their use. Wherever that is done, the church is unfree. She is free where she stands alone in the service of her Lord, who seeks *all* men, who will open the door to God and the door to fellow men to all. We are all free when and to the extent that we stand in obedience to the love of Christ. "Stand in this freedom!" This means: pursue this line further, from Bethlehem and Golgotha through the door which leads to God and one's neighbor. Do not let yourself be derailed by care, anxiety, desire. Let this freedom be sent ever and again by God's Word. Let yourself be led back to it ever and again. That is the most real and the most helpful thing that could be said to us for the new year. Let us be aroused again and again by this call, hold it in our spirit, let it put us to work. Then much else will be unimportant. Then we go comforted into the future, whatever it may be. Then we have always a meaningful task. Then truly something has changed in the world. Then will praise and thanksgiving be our final word. AMEN.

The Question of the Meaning of Life

by Helmut Thielicke *

(Scripture: Mark 10:17ff)

How does it happen that all of a sudden there rises up in a person the quest for the eternal life, for the fundamental? It may be some young person or other, as in this story, who is suddenly driven hither and yon by this issue. Not always does it rise in such a form that the rubric "eternal life" is appropriate. He may put the question under another heading entirely. Perhaps the young man spoke in this way: Who is really right in the use of his life? Albert Schweitzer, who let go a great academic career, who has no interest in a dreamhouse, who instead went into the bush to spend his time with ugly sicknesses among the natives, *or* is it the successful businessman with his Mercedes 300 and his inlaid swimming pool? Is it the real thing when a man performs a real service

* Helmut Thielicke is Professor at the University of Hamburg. Dr. Thielicke was a cofounder of Bad Ball Evangelical Academy in 1945.

and buries himself in it, *or* when he has prestige, career, success and, in extreme cases, appears on the front page of an illustrated magazine? What is it that's fundamental, about which in the final analysis everything else turns?

When the young man asks in this way, he has—more unconsciously than deliberately—put the question of eternal life.

But the older person asks the question too. Perhaps he asks himself this question. Let's say that he has just retired. His place at the office is now filled by another. No one calls on him any more. He can sleep until noon. No one cares. The old colleagues are nice to him when he looks in. But he senses that when he is there he just holds things up: he isn't important to them any more. And now the older person asks himself this: What did I live for? Did I bring something essential into my barns, on which I can now live and be filled? Or did I deceive myself into thinking that production was the only important thing, so now I am abandoned and redundant, vegetating and accomplishing *nothing* more? When the older person suffers this shock of being eliminated, he too—more unconsciously than deliberately—puts the question of eternal life, i.e., the question of life's real meaning which one can miss so tragically.

To what end do I really live? That is the question which cannot be avoided.

Of course you can fail to hear it—good night, what a racket we have in our ears! I'm happy enough when I've just dug my way through the daily task at the desk. I don't have time to think about that over-the-hill, that final *goal* at which this is all to end someday. That's a luxury for loafers or a hobby for the morbid. And yet, as Albert Einstein said one time, we live in a time of perfect mediocrity and confused ends. We have refrigerators and TVs. We have social institutions that lighten life and make it more certain. But those are all technical means which should make life more worthwhile. What do we want of them all? With what oppressive perfection and intelligence a TV or tape-recorder works! But what sentimental drivel appears on the screens with the help of these intelligent machines! Was this tremendous technical effort really necessary in order to express such breath-taking banalities? As Dr. Einstein concluded, is this insipid stammering the goal to which such technical perfection leads us?

Doesn't this evidence of failure—that is, that we have no goal any more, that in all of it we cannot discover the meaning of life—produce our boredom? The comfort of our world is only attractive at first. A moment later we've taken it for granted and it becomes insipid. And when the juvenile delinquents demonstrate life in somewhat aberrational forms, it is only a symptom of this boredom.

But the pious, churchgoing Christian can also put this question about eternal life. The rich young ruler of our story is rather like a member of the official board, a delegate to the assembly. He is prominent in denominational affairs. And it may come to pass for such a man that all of a sudden he has to ask, "Where do I find some real vitality in all this dust of dogmatics? Where do I find something which overpowers me and is stronger than the depression which comes upon me from time to time? How many times have I heard the Christmas message, 'Behold, I bring you great joy!' I know all these texts by heart. And yet I've never been swept along. I've never been lifted out of my seat. And I've never been really joyful and aroused either. How often I've heard at communion, 'Thy sins are forgiven thee.' And I've taken it seriously and wanted to make a new beginning. But on the next day the same old treadmill started up again. And I've started all over again with what I bitterly repented at the altar. Where is then that well-known life from God, that draws one to it and molds him anew? Perhaps my query isn't first about 'truth' at all. I'm not so elevated as all this. For me the issue is love, a reality where I sense that I must give in, which makes clear to me with a single blow what's really important! I'm stuck in the religious routine and I thrash the empty straw of Christian verbalization. One can't say it out loud," or so perhaps the churchgoing Christian thinks, "but sometimes the whole thing is a load around my neck."

In this condition—and it is the condition of all of us—the rich young ruler comes to Jesus. It sometimes happens that this question is more important to a person than the problem of the bill due and the growling stomach after a hearty meal. That was the way of it with this young man, as he ran to Jesus and threw himself down before him.

One must see the picture clearly in order to assess its significance. Jesus was surrounded by people. For the most part they were simple people from the masses. It seems a bit staged when a man in tailored, aristocratic clothes appears among these social outsiders. But he didn't just appear: he threw himself down before Jesus. It was a sensation! One goes to such lengths only when the issue is nothing less than life itself. Only when one is up to the neck in something will he cease to care what impression he makes on other people or whether he perhaps is compromising himself. Sometimes today someone will push himself forward in the pressure before the ticket windows at a major football game, when he is so obsessed with the notion that he must see the game that he doesn't care at all whether other people in the queue think him a boor.

Thus the rich young man didn't care at all what was around him or before him. There was only one man, Jesus, for him and only one question, which had become his fate. And what happened?

One might think that Jesus and his disciples would have been pleased. At last a man from the ruling class of his nation, and not always and forever the little people! At last someone who wanted no alms, no minor conversation without bindingness, no mere fencing; at last someone who wasn't filled with physical pains and woes, seeking only a miracle-worker! *At last, at last a man with a fundamental question!* Thus many a counselor, with waiting room filled with people with the routine, pedestrian affairs, loses himself in the wish that just *once* someone would come to him during the week —*just one!*—who would put such a question to him, who would be driven toward the fundamental by a great unrest.

"Good Teacher," said the man, "what must I do to inherit eternal life?"—Say something to me about the meaning of my life, for I have gone astray in it, and then command what you will! I will carry any burden, even an eleventh or a twelfth commandment for the elite (*noblesse oblige*!)! If I can only have the feeling that I am in harmony with myself and with my inner direction! I can't bear life any more if I have no pitch to tune to. I am lost in meaninglessness. And don't be misled by the fact that outwardly things go well with me. Good Master—please!

And shouldn't Jesus now lift him from the ground and say to him: "Thank you for coming with this question. I'm glad that you are a seeker."

But Jesus reacted in a way strangely different from what we expect. Actually he had only a "cold shower" for this young seeker. He refused to be called—was that really the first word spoken?—"Good Master" by him. "No one is good but God alone."

Why did Jesus say that? Why at that very moment?

Obviously the rich young ruler saw in Jesus a kind of teacher who had certain standard answers for helping him get straight in his problem of life. The young man seemed to think he could pass God by and find a solution to this problem. Jesus was, for him, a kind of "Dear Abby". . . . Look once at the readers' questions which appear in these agony columns of our newspapers. They are all on the same level: "I suffer from loneliness. How can I come to living, human contacts? My man has left me and run off. How can I save my marriage? No one dances with me. How can I be attractive?"

Now Abby and her colleagues often have something quite helpful to say. They give helpful advice as to what can be changed, and the warmhearted desire to be helpful can be sensed too. But of course such a doctor of souls would be asked too much if it went beyond tinkering a bit with the symptoms, if one were to expect a basic healing. But then, good advice and a bit of correction in the style of life are not to be despised.

But Jesus handled things quite differently with this young man. He denied the entire level of relations on which one works with "good suggestions." Anyone who lets Jesus operate must allow a sharp knife to get at his roots. If you only want an easy recipe for our life questions, so he informs the young man who kneels before him and looks at him with burning anticipation, then you have come to the wrong address. Therefore please don't say "Good Master" or "Most Honored Doctor" to me, as though I had such easy answers as to how one comes to terms with life. The questions of your life can't be solved as long as you avoid the *one* and *decisive* issue: namely, how you stand with God. In him alone is the good which you seek. He is the end which you pursue and the meaning for which you are longing. "No one is good but God alone."

Perhaps it is "Greek" to one or the other of us that God enters not only the sector of the pious inner life, but appears here as a very real factor which penetrates conclusively into everything which is unmastered, questionable, and troublesome in our life—that God has to do with our marriage, with our professional life, with our loneliness, and with our anxieties. In order to understand our story we must reflect a bit on this question.

Why do I feel lonesome and misunderstood? Most of the time I don't let this question come to the surface. The TV is there in the evening and tomorrow I'm going to a party. Of course I feel that these things occupy only the outward, the periphery of my life, but nevertheless one forgets himself somewhat in the midst of them. But then one day the TV is out of order or I have the sniffles and can't go out. Then I have to be alone. Then I don't know where to begin with myself, and the emptiness of my life depresses me and brings me down into the pit. Who then is really with me? Who then would really stand by me, if I really fell into the ditch? Where would there really be an empty place, an unfulfilled assignment, if I fell out? Perhaps I then dial the time service of the telephone company, as someone recently reported to me, just to hear a human voice.

How different it would be if I could pray, if there were then a "Thou" there who said to me: "Fear not," or "I have called you by name, you are mine," or "Peace be with thee." Doesn't my loneliness have something to do with the fact, really, that I have lost God? And wouldn't it be different with my marriage and my friendships, which I don't have and want so much, if I were more relaxed, if I were more peaceful within, if I were less distrustful and cramped inside? In short, if I came out of the peace of God, and if there radiated from me the freedom of a man that knew himself cared for by God and blessed with a liberated conscience? Wouldn't everything look quite different if *this* question, the question of *God,* were straightened out in me?

And this is the reason for this remarkable "cold shower"

with which Jesus met the overheated life problems of the young man. You see, I am no advice-to-the-lovelorn columnist; I have no universal recipes. You must set the foundations of life anew. You must begin with the question who and what God is to be to you.

Now only one step seemed to be lacking for a brave religious discussion to begin, and then it would end like most discussions of this sort, that is, with a hung jury. But Jesus did not discuss: he came with unapologetic and very binding address. To have to do with God. . . . That is no pious sentiment, but means to be placed face to face with his Commandments; that means, to enter the field of unlimited liability. Then he simply listed the Commandments: Do not kill, do not commit adultery, etc. He means to say, take God seriously, that is all. Through this experiment you will discover "meaning" all by yourself, and come near to eternal life.

At this, the rich young ruler was certainly very shocked: *I* beat myself with the final issues of life, and he addresses me like a primary teacher with the little lessons of the catechism. He gave me a bottle of milk when I needed bread. But I have problems, Jesus of Nazareth (*my* problems are *important!*), and you take me back to kindergarten.

But the young man only *thinks* that, without saying it. He has enough self-control to respond with an answer which only hints at the disappointment: ". . . all these have I observed from my youth." I have taken God seriously, believe me. And yet I am come to a frontier where I don't know how to go on. All those things didn't bring me peace of mind. If I thought I could come clean with God in that way, I wouldn't be here!

In fact, this rich young man is more than just someone "interested spiritually," a mere seeker who is—like Faust—very happy indeed that he hasn't found anything finally obligating, but can remain at the level of spiritual adventure and can fish in the tank of the uncommitted. No: this man is unapologetic about himself. He not only played with religious philosophy a bit, and with the question of God, but he took Him so seriously that he declared his bankruptcy here before strange eyes and half publicly. Indeed, the compromising situation in which he put himself left him totally unmoved.

But—and that is now the question—doesn't this man live in an amazing self-deception? Is it then truly possible to say so simply: "I have kept the Commandments of God"? There may be something like that in our daily routine, as viewed from the outside. There has perhaps been no really major adultery, and a man hasn't stolen any silver spoons either. But hasn't he ever noticed what really goes on inside himself, what happens *behind* the curtains of his outwardly correct behavior, how he has hated and murdered his brother in his mind even while he gave him his hand? And how many times—not outwardly evident, of course!—did he rob his neighbor of his possessions, of those things he wanted for himself? Adalbert Stifter wrote once in one of his letters: "Every one of us has a tiger-like disposition, and no one knows what wickedness he might commit when aroused, if all restraints were removed." Hadn't the rich young ruler ever noticed what—unnoticed by human eye but well marked by God—rumbled and raged in his heart, and how he had sabotaged the Ten Commandments one by one and systematically? Isn't he a rank dilettante toward the problem of God, doesn't he have a beam in his eye when he overlooks all that and can say with the resounding voice of conviction: I, I have kept all the Commandments of God from my youth. I have always taken God seriously.

Certainly this is the sore point in his life. But now comes the amazing: Jesus did not rage against what this man had done wrong and where he had erred. It says quite simply, before the meeting went a bit further, "and Jesus looking upon him loved him." It seems to me this is one of the most comforting passages in the whole New Testament. Jesus doesn't love me first when I do something right and when I am perfect and have everything in order. Long before it comes to this level I *am* loved. He always has the initiative. Perhaps I am a young person who doesn't even know where to begin with Jesus. All I have is a great hunger and thirst and many questions in my heart. And because I'm very helpless, I poke around in Nietzsche, repeat a couple of verses by Gottfried Benn, nibble a bit in Sartre, and even crib a little— and why not—from the New Testament. Let's see if something strikes my fancy, if something speaks to me! What else should I do in my helplessness except let everything pass in review before me? And while I do that (perhaps over a cigarette, lying on the rug, or slouching on the couch), and while everything is still cloudy and confused, Jesus stands there opposite me, beholds me and loves me. Everything that

I do—and even if it is utterly false, and even though I persist in pushing the wrong buttons—everything that I do is surrounded and lifted up and carried by this love. I never escape from the gravitational field of this loving glance.

That must be known and held fast to when in the next moment Jesus goes over to the attack. For he does that. We must accept the fact that Jesus can also be hard and that he faces us with solid surfaces, and that he has nothing, but nothing, to do with the feminine, prettified picture surmounted by a halo that Christian bad taste has made of him. As he took the offensive against the rich young ruler, we must always remember the words in the background: "Jesus looking upon him loved him." The offensive itself consisted of a single verse: "You lack one thing; go, sell what you have, and give it to the poor, and you will have treasure in heaven; and come, follow me."

It is amazing how with Jesus there is always just one thing at stake: "It is meet"; "You lack one thing." Any one of us could count on his fingers a list of indefinite length, of all kinds of things lacking to fill up his happiness, things that seem essential to him. But Jesus is the great simplifier. He reduces everything that we hope and fear for to the first point: Fundamentally I have only *one* problem, only *one* sure point, only *one* possibility of salvation. According to what I undertake with this one and fundamental thing, everything else falls into place.

Thus he said to the rich young ruler, too: "You lack one thing." But how striking the one thing is that is said to be lacking: "go, sell what you have!" The young man wasn't ready for that. Such a sweeping claim was too much for him. For the second time, cold water was thrown on him. He belongs to the educated classes and immediately begins to calculate: Where would we end up if everyone carried through such a sale? Isn't that crazy? If I should sell everything in order to be more perfect, then wouldn't I make the others whom I have aroused to buy even more *im*perfect? Then the other party to the sale would have to pay the moral costs for my impoverishment! What child's play. . . . Or— he figures further: if all were now to sell what they had, where would be the purchasers? What kind of a crazy economy would we have then? That is simply unrealistic, Jesus of Nazareth. You can't lead a man away from responsibility and good sense.

And now the young man stands up, disappointed, confused, and uncertain. How he had trusted this man and how serious he had been about it all! He would have been willing to add to the Ten Commandments, which he had kept from his youth, yet an eleventh and a twelfth with yet more difficult ethical proscriptions. He would have been ready to pray for hours in a darkened room or to fulfil a fast day twice a week, if it could have brought him closer to eternal life. Yes, he thinks, I'm ready for the most serious effort. Instead of that he comes to me in the name of God with this nonsense to take away from me everything that God's blessing has brought in. He is attacking like an enthusiast the whole order of society.

But doesn't the rich young ruler deceive himself a second time? Isn't it clear that he doesn't want to hear and understand what Jesus has to say to him secretly with his remarkable requirement? What then did Jesus want to say to him?

Evidently what he meant was this: No doubt, beloved, you have taken God seriously and you have made things hard for yourself. Therefore I ask you as a thoroughgoing seeker if you have taken God seriously in a *real* and *radical* sense. Aren't you really interested in religion because you want peace of mind? Or because life seemed shallow and empty and you sought here a lift to your emotions? Or because you noticed that the reputation of being a pious man brought social benefits, and you sought to elevate the social prestige, yours through your property, a little higher? Wasn't God in the final analysis just a means to an end [the way we gladly use him today to oppose the witchery of the East with a Christian ideology, or to shore up the Christian West spiritually]? Haven't you built religion into your life in this way, very earnestly, very uprightly? Certainly. But has God meant any more to you than a pious extra, a final polishing of your standard of living, a pious style of life? Examine yourself once more, Jesus seems to be saying, by putting it to the test. Are you prepared to give up everything for God? Only then, when you can do that, will it be evident that he is the one and all to you and that you trust him *utterly* and take him seriously *without any reservation.*

In that remarkable requirement of Jesus that he should sell everything that he had, there was also the requirement that an experiment be made. Lay everything that you hold valuable and precious in life on the left tray of your scale. Put in this tray your cultivated way of life, on which you count so much (and I haven't anything against that, either!). Put in, too, your friendships, your social prestige, your spiritual gifts. And then place in the right tray the weight which God has in your life. And now watch which of the trays sinks in the balance. That is the most serious test, that is the deadly experiment. And now it is evident that the tray which holds everything that I hold precious and dear in life sinks, and has the greater weight.

Then the rich young ruler stood up and went away grieved, for he had great possessions and was a gifted man and the left balance of his life was very heavy. He wanted religion as an additional flavor. In addition to everything that enriched his life he wanted also the inner possession of spiritual depth and breadth. Therefore in the final analysis he was not seeking eternal life. He sought God as an elixir of life to take away the boredom of wealth and give him inner vitality. God was to be a final, crowning addition to his life. He was to be a means to improve his life, but he was not to be the one and only life itself.

But God cannot be bought at this price.

God cannot be addressed by the one who hasn't put the harshness of the all-or-nothing to himself. Therefore it may be that the rich and gifted are the ones in gravest danger. A well-laden camel cannot pass through the needle's eye of the city gate. Sometimes a poorer and less gifted person has it easier just to raise his hand that God's gift may come. Or a child has it easier, because he has nothing himself and makes no demands.

"Then who can be saved?" the disciples asked astonished.

Aren't we all of us somewhere rich men, that is, people who have something in their lives of which they are proud and on which they have fixed their hearts? Don't I stand in the scale myself when I want to press toward God—and not just with all kinds of dark drives, the normal impulses of my heart, at all, but also with the greatness of my life, with my gifts, with my spiritual quality and the *élan* which carries me along?

Yes, that is it, and just that is the secret of the kingdom of God.

And that is the greatness too. Is it not great and appealing that at *this* gate of entrance and at *this* needle's eye no one is greater than another, that here all are equal—persons from whom God must first lift the burdens *and* the gifts of their lives, that we become as children who can only receive gifts?

As Jesus Christ hung on the cross, as he had no one and nothing left, as his followers were scattered to the winds and even his garment had fallen into the hands of the gambling and drinking company of soldiers, he was nearest to his father. Then there was nothing more which could stand between him and his father; and he bowed his head and commended himself into the hands of the eternal. Everyone must go through this death and change who desires eternal life.

Of course we can't do it. We cannot release our own clenched fists from that of ours which we grasp so strenuously. "With men it is impossible . . ." God knows, it *is* impossible. But "all things are possible with God."

The rich young ruler didn't get what he wanted and he

went away grieved. We do not know his later history. Did perhaps the One who looked upon him and loved him bring him at the end to himself? Was it perhaps the last attempted escape before he was finally brought alive?

So it is with you. Whether you now hope to find the solution of your questions with this Nazarene, or whether you are the disappointed who shake the head in amazement and leave this service, one thing is called out to you: Jesus Christ has looked upon and loved you. And now turn where you will. There is no spot unreached by this love, and there is no place which these arms do not surround.

Christ as Meaning

by James A. Pike *

(Scripture: John 1:1ff)

I would like you to imagine with me tonight, that in place of these first three or four pews (and obviously we need to leave them in place tonight) and in place of all of you who are sitting here, we have before us a large oriental rug of varying colors and bold design—yellows, reds, greens, blues, whites—and that on this rug, right under the watchful eye of the Rector, is a small moth trying to have dinner. This moth is not only very small; he is very allergic, that is, very sensitive to his immediate surrounding.

At the moment, he is in a deep blue section and, being very small, as he looks out, everything is blue; in fact, he gets "the blues." He is depressed, downcast; he has no interest in anything; he loses his appetite. In this state he has waddled over to a section that is all yellow, and as he turns that way it is yellow all the way to the horizon. He looks

* James A. Pike is Bishop of California in the Protestant Episcopal Church. This was the first sermon preached in the Bishop's Preaching Mission to the churches of San Mateo County, 1961.

up, he takes hope, he takes courage, he makes new plans, he gains an appetite and nibbles away like a buffalo. But now, digesting his rather heavy dinner, he has backed up to a deep red section, and as he is engulfed by this section of deep red, it has a strange effect on his unconscious depths, and he tends to regurgitate all his hatreds of brother moths, and by a very natural psychosomatic connection he soon has dyspepsia. Now, distressed again, he has found his way into a white section—very white indeed (things are kept very clean around this church)—and against that pure white he feels smaller than ever; in fact, he feels guilty: he feels wrong for all those awful hateful thoughts that he had, and he begins to say his prayers.

Well, time will not permit my taking you through the entire spectrum of the rainbow. I think enough has been said to suggest that this moth is headed for a nervous breakdown. Now, were you the moth's psychoanalyst, I think you would suggest that the moth fly up here, or up to this chancel arch and get a view of the whole rug, see what the design is—the relationship of the colors and the scheme of things. Then the moth could return to the rug and with complete equanimity "make out three squares a day." Notice three things before we roll up the rug and let you people sit down again. First of all, the rug did not change at all, depending upon where the moth was examining the rug. When the moth was on the rug and when the moth was up here, the rug was the same (i.e., the rug didn't change, but *the meaning of the rug for the moth* changed, depending on the perspective from which the moth looked at the rug). Second, the moth by now would have decided that up there was a better perspective, a better vantage point, from which to view the rug than looking at the rug from the rug. And why? Because from one of these other places the rug makes more sense. And living on the rug is healthier than when one only looks at the rug from the rug. Third, when the moth was looking at the rug from the rug, he was not in some neutral or objective position in relation to the rug: it, too, was a vantage point, a viewpoint, perspective, a selected place.

This leads me to the nature of religion. *Religion is perspective,* religion as not just a part of the rug of life. Depending on your past experience with religion, you may think it is the blue part, the gold-yellow part, the deep red part—or whatever; but it is not just a part of the rug of life—it is the vantage point from which we look at the whole of life. And that religion is soundest which makes the most sense out of all of experienced reality. In any case, we will have a religion: even on the rug crawling around on his tummy the moth is looking at the rug from some point of view. There is no such thing as neutrality or objectivity about this—everybody lives life out looking at things from some vantage point, has some working premises, has some priority scale of values: some things are more important than others.

All of these are judgments not proven but taken by faith, whether one has a formal religion or not. With many, these judgments are made unconsciously without careful analysis as to where one really does stand. Sometimes persons profess to be Christians, or even Episcopalians, and yet make their value judgments as though they were natives from some Pacific island. So, in any case, we're going to have a perspective on life. The reason why for many of us life is shattering as an experience, unreliable from crisis to crisis—unstable; the reason why there is so much anxiety, fear and frustration and despair, is that persons do not have an adequate perspective on the whole, do not have a vantage point where they can see and know the meaning of things—a meaning so that they may make right decisions and have consistent behavior and responsible living, with a confidence through one's days.

There are many religions—some good, some bad. Since I say everyone has one, that automatically suggests that I don't call all religion good. Marxism is a religion—it's a way to understand reality taken on faith—and it's not good. "The religious" does not automatically equal "the good." There are very bad religions in the world—there are some that are worse than others; and there are none, because of the human elements in them, that are perfect. But the choice one must make is for a perspective. One will have one anyway; and the claim of Christianity can rest only on the claim that it is the soundest perspective, namely, that the rug of life makes more sense from this perspective.

In connection with this, I'm talking tonight, on the first of our three times together, on *Christ as Meaning*. I hope you will come back because we will by no means exhaust the role of Christ in our lives under this one heading; but it's where we have to start. This is not only for those who perhaps have not been found of Him or for whom He is not very real, but for the "faithful" who often are very loyal to the church, but who are not very well acquainted with the Lord of the church. Sometimes we are so busy with church affairs that we have very little time for the Head of the household.

Christ is meaning. How do we know that there's anything beyond what we can see and weigh and touch and count? A consistent position that there *isn't,* we call secularism—that there isn't any more. Secularism comes from the same Latin root which we find in the traditional ending to many of our prayers in the Western tradition—the Latin ending is *per omnia saecular saeculorum* translated variously in the Prayer Book, "throughout all ages of ages" (literally) or "forever and ever" or "world without end." Now that same root *saeculum* gives us our word "secularism." The word *saeculum* means an age. Secularism means "this ageism," means "this-is-all-there-is-ism";—it means "there-ain't-anymore-ism." That's it: you've had it. Now, *per omnia saecular saeculorum* means that in addition to man and things there is God, in addition to history and time there is eternity, in addition to "is's" there are "oughts"; in addition to flesh there is spirit. It's more roomy, a bigger perspective than secularism. Secularism has decided automatically that there isn't any more and that if someone thinks there is something more, then the problem is how to explain that in the narrow limits of what is, there are these illusions in their minds that there is more. If you start from the secularist's premise, as did Sigmund Freud (and this would have been characteristic of a nineteenth-century intellectual), it has nothing to do with the soundness of his system of psychotherapy, but simply with his own working religious premise that there isn't any more. So naturally he had to try to explain why so many people thought there was some more. What in their unconscious mind caused them to think there was a God? Well, he said, it's the projection out of the unconscious of the love of father, the need for an authoritative figure. The projection of that, blown up big on the screen, that is God. A modern Christian psychiatrist, using exactly Sigmund Freud's categories, believing that there is a God, had the opposite problem to work on. Why do people think there isn't? What is atheism? he said. He says atheism is often the projection of father-hatred. Now, I'm not here to argue the case for either of those gentlemen; but we see that the system works both ways, depending on where you start your thinking. If you think there's a God, then you try to figure out why some people are atheists, and if you think there isn't, you try to figure out why some people think there is a God. But the secularist's mind has assumed in advance that *there can't be any more* and has assumed as an operating principle that there need be no more and that life can be dealt with and contained within the limits of the tangible, the weighable, the countable, and so forth. The trouble with secularism is that it isn't roomy enough for the actual experience of life and for relationships and responses of which we are capable.

There was once a good king Procrustes who was a very genial host except he had a very odd habit. After his guest was in bed, a butler came and examined the situation, and if a man were too short for the bed, a couple of house chiropractors came and stretched him out; and if he were too long for the bed, a couple of house carpenters came and sawed him off. This, needless to say, is a very free translation from the Greek. Now, ever since, we have referred to what is called a "Procrustean bed" one that isn't big enough for the person who's going to be in it. Well, secularism is a Procrustean bed because it isn't big enough to contain those capacities of human response to a great big roomy world, a bigger one than the unbeliever ever knows.

When I was in college there was a strange illusion around that those who held this narrower, cramped Procrustean point of view were the broad-minded students, while those who held the roomier point of view of the general Christian tradition were narrow-minded students. Just a confusion of words, I know; but it sometimes confused the freshmen. But if one would decide for Christianity on a sound basis, not just on a basis of how one was born, or tradition, or the comforts it brings, or if one enjoys the ladies' guild or something, but really comes down to it and decides not only for Christianity but for Christ, it would be that in these terms this understanding of the meaning of things, the purpose and measure of our hopes is sounder, is roomier, it gives more chance to be a whole person than otherwise.

Now, what is this over-all understanding? And why is it plausible? Why does it make more sense than alternatives? We can start, I think, with looking at ourselves. I am quite different from a horse or a cucumber—principally in this: I have certain capacities of personality which enable me to transcend myself, to be more than me.

Now, let me illustrate one of these. I am in my present, I am right here with you, I'm fully in this moment, I hope; but I still have all my past, much of which I can recall. I have all of that as a present reality for working purposes; I use all that by way of experience for making decisions. Further, I can look to the future, and on the basis of the past and present; and, with common experience that I understand beyond my own experience, I can make certain projections of what may be: I can plan what I may do in the future and it comes off. A few weeks ago I knew I would be here tonight—that was part of my then present; I somehow was able to span past, present and future. I can make decisions and project myself into situations.

I can even change *me*. Some years ago I was dressing and happened to catch a glimpse of myself sideways in a full-length mirror and I then knew what my wife had been saying was right. Hence I became one of the first users of that interesting product known as Metrecal. Well, now, believe it or not, *I changed the shape of me*. You might say, what has that got to do with religion? Well, it says a very important and unique thing about a human being: *he doesn't have to be the way he is.* A man can look at himself and change himself, not only physically but in other ways: mental, moral—everything. I use this obvious example to show that man has something that no dog or no rock has. And I have another quality. I can articulate or express myself, relate to others and carry my thoughts and perceptions outside of me to others: I can *reveal* myself. In fact, we would regard this as one of the higher, more sensitive qualities of a man, evaluating him by the degree to which he can do that very thing.

Now, why am I talking about myself and about you? Because if at this late stage of the evolutionary progress something like *this* comes along, then those qualities, those factors must have been in the mix all along, or they wouldn't appear by evolution. Certainly, we were evolved; but whatever is evolved has to already have been in the mix. No stream rises higher than its source; nothing new comes into the whole mix of the universe. For those who know something about physics (as I do not), I cite the Second Law of Thermodynamics. In fact, unscientific indeed would be a view of the world which said that without any great Mind or Creator, without any great Force or Personality who had all these things, from lower species finally it has evolved up to us, where these qualities of transcendence of mind and will and articulation and all the other human qualities suddenly emerge out of nothing. That isn't scientific—that's rabbits out of hats: that's magic, not science.

In other words, by looking at ourselves, we can see that at least this much was in the mix from the beginning. *At least* there was mind and will and articulation, revelatory qualities. At least this. Well, this is why it is more sensible to believe that there has been and is and will be a God than that there is not. It is the more plausible of the two views. Now, if I am revelatory at my best, then we must say God is at least that—or I wouldn't be that. Thus it is not surprising that God all along has been trying to reveal Himself to us:

that He may be in a person-to-person relationship with us, because person-to-person relationship is a reflection of the highest capacity of personal development. God is at least capable of that.

And this very thing He has been doing in many, many ways—through wise men of all times who have tried to teach men to rise from the old familiar lies, through those who by art or poetry or music or design have lifted men out of the tawdry and stirred their poetic imagination, through those who have condemned the mores when the mores were crippling to the spirit of man, from those who were the prophets, the rocks in the shoe, the sore thumbs, the bulls in the china shop of their own day, safely ensconced in their new generation in stained-glass windows, but not very convenient to have around at the time, through the intimations of the soul in solitary meditation, through the inspiration of corporate worship of all times and places, yes, through the philosophers and religious thinkers of all traditions outside and inside the Judeo-Christian one—yes, wherever men were seeking the truth, the *Truth was seeking them!*

The conviction that this is the case was expressed in the glorious passage that opens the Fourth Gospel. It says, just as I say, that God by very nature is articulate and expressive —"wordy," if you wish. (We are at our most fully developed stage. That's just what we read in the sixth chapter of John.) "In the beginning"—the Greek for that (*en arche*) doesn't mean just "in the beginning" as a matter of time; it means also "as a fundamental matter," "in the nature of things," "at the bottom of things." So we read—"In the

beginning was the Word, and the Word was with God . . ."
In other words, God's *very nature* requires expression, communication. Then we see that He has been expressing Himself and revealing Himself through the evolving creation. The beauty of the world with its very apparent order, the way things hold together, the way things work from the elaborate design of the human eye, to that of the constellations and their courses, this has and does reveal Him to us. The chapter goes on to say that "all things were made through him"—and in this way He's revealing himself. And then it goes on to speak of the way God works in all cultures, in all frames of reference and thought. This, it says, and all this refers to the Word, the revelatory quality of God, the revelatory attribute, "the true Light that enlightens every man was coming into the world"—not just Jews and Christians or Episcopalians, it says—*every man*. When the light comes, it's God's light coming. A man thinks he's found an answer; actually, he was found. As he looked, light came. This is true of the workings of the mind of man as enlightened by God.

Now, so far this chapter sets forth a very broad gauge kind of religion. Those who think that God has only worked through the Christian church regard notions like those I've just expressed as overly liberal; but I remind you that this is not some modern liberal Protestant thinking; it's right there in the Fourth Gospel, plainly stated. Our God is a very, very big God and He is not confined in the fulfillment of His purposes to any earthly visible institution. And certainly not to any one of the portions of the church. The pastoral letter which you will soon hear sent out by our House of Bishops after the Detroit General Convention says something like this: that it would not appear that God has entrusted His whole task in the world to the Protestant Episcopal Church. But, in the next part of the text comes a narrowing, a sharp focusing which does assert the uniqueness of the Christian faith. Up till now the author has been talking pretty much like a very objective professor of comparative religion—and, fine, he should. But now, just as on a sunny day you suddenly take a big magnifying glass and put it against a piece of paper and something very definitely comes right from the same source again, the sun is not changed—it's the same—but the result has changed because there's a focusing. We come to this great text: "And the Word [the Word—this same eternal quality of God always acting and always expressing itself in many ways—this same reality of God] became flesh, and dwelt among us, (and we have beheld his glory . . .)"

Some people have wondered why God would reveal Himself in a particular man, in a particular place, at a particular time. Why wouldn't He simply be acting *in general*. The answer is, He *is* acting in general, but His acting in a particular place through a particular man, in a particular period of history is the very way you would expect a revelatory God to act, at the right time and place. Why? Because compared with all of these other modes of communication—the created evolving order, the intimations in the hearts of men, the learning of sages and prophets and statesmen, and so forth—there is nothing like a face-to-face confrontation in terms of human personality. People can correspond for years but meeting face to face is the ultimate in communication, as you well know. God has been corresponding with us, He has been throwing out hints, He's been drawing us pictures, and then finally at the right time He translates himself into the language of human life. Why the right time? I borrow that phrase from Paul. In the Greek there are two words for time—one is *kairos* and the other is *chronos*. *Chronos* (as in chronometer or chronomology or in "what time is it?") is a neutral kind of word. *Kairos* is not a neutral word, it's a charged word. As in the phrase "*that* was the time." It is that word that Paul uses when he talks about the time of the coming of our Lord, Jesus Christ. It was the right time. Why? Because for the first time in the history of mankind you have a people who, slowly and patiently tutored by God, come to an ethical monotheism; that is, realize that there is one final overarching reality, that we are involved in the destiny of His total plan, and that we are to be responsible persons under judgment of that God. This was the first time in human history that there was developed a people whose God was not a kept god to be used by them for their purposes—to head their legions, to bear them out, to hurt the enemy, and so forth—to be called in as you would call in a genie to meet the situation —one who was always on your side and always against the other side. Instead of that, cutting through all, you find a God who might very well be for the other side and against your own nation and people because you're being judged and the other side is "the rod of his anger." He is God who is over and above national hopes and personal ambitions—a God who is not to be used but for whom we are to be used.

Secondly, they had an expectancy of His continuing revelation—an expectancy indeed of His coming in the flesh to be made known as the Messiah. Why? Why is that of value? First, so that mankind may know what a man really is. Hence, tomorrow night we'll talk about Christ as Pattern. Christ as true man—the Man. And, second, what God is really like toward us, particularly when we've not been the men we ought to be. Hence, we will talk Tuesday night about Christ as Saviour. That we may know what we're supposed to be like and what God is like toward us, is the reason Jesus came.

It was at the *right time* because, first, finally, patiently and slowly God had raised up such a people who could understand such a thing when it came. There is no use for the Messiah to come when He is not expected—when the questions have not been asked for which He gives the answers (there is nothing more irrelevant than answers to questions no one has ever asked). The questions were right—the understanding of a world in which there is a living God and one who expects something of us was deep in these people and so the time was right from that point of view. Second, for the first time human thought had developed into a logical pattern through the Greek philosophy that there was a way of communicating meaning as there never had been in history before. And, third, through the Roman domination of the civilized world communications were relatively rapid and it was possible for the light of meaning quickly to come to the civilized world and then from that to the whole of the world.

If Paul a few decades later could see, as he did, that this was the right time for God to make His great break-through, all the more now looking back two thousand years we can see that this was the time. Any time God chose to come would be a special time, and any person through whom He would come would be a special person: that is "the scandal" referred to in the Bible. We're put off by the idea that God would be all that particular; but God would be just that particular and that vivid and that real with us if He really wanted to communicate with us, and as I say, by his very nature He does. At the foundation of things is the Word, the communicating, speaking God, a God who talks. Not simply a mystical idea, or a body of principle, but a living God.

Some people say, "But I can't think of Him as a person; it seems that that's being very anthropomorphic, that is, very manlike, a making of God in our own image—we're trying to make Him just a bigger version of me." Yes, in a way that's true. We can't think of anything except in the terms of the minds we have, and these are limited minds, and we can only think of things as analogies of what we see around us and know. It is from these qualities indeed that we can grasp something of the meaning of God's love. Indeed, this is one of the reasons why in good Christian education programs we try to involve the whole family in every redemptive activity; a child in a home where he hasn't experienced much love can go pretty dead in a classroom when they're talking about the love of God. The word "love" doesn't carry much if he hasn't known much love. A person can't understand much about the forgiveness of God if he hasn't known much forgiveness in his home or family or school—for him it's an empty word. It's as we can see these things in our own human lives that we can even imagine what God is like. So to that degree we are making Him in our own image. But, on the other hand, the very fact that we have those qualities in ourselves by which we can love and plan and live responsibly and relate ourselves one to another and express ourselves leads us to the knowledge that all must be in the universe, that the universe is shot through with those things or they never would have emerged, and, therefore, I conclude that God must be at least personal or I would not be. Therefore, it does no good to say, well, I can think of Him as a great Force, because that's to make Him into merely an "it" and an "it" is a less thing than a "he." In fact, we use things—we buy up things and put them together and make them into other things—we can burn things. In fact, in ethics perhaps the greatest sin is to use persons as things—you'll find that covers most of the evils that we do to each other—using a person as a thing which you can manipulate or step on to get where you want to get for what you want to achieve. So, God is certainly not less than me; therefore, He is at least a Person. But He is obviously more than me and so we must always throw in the "at least." That's why feebly we try to express this by a capital H—we know He's at least a "He," that "He" is more than "he" and that's about as far as we can go.

But we cannot by human speculation, even of the most refined and thoughtful sort, capture the nature of God. We cannot capture Him in our imaginings or philosophizing any more than we could capture Him in a box. And when we have said all we have to say, we still don't know too much about God; that is, on our own when we try to think these things through, taking into our experience the experience of others. In the end we have to say in the words of the Book of Job, "As touching the Almighty, we cannot find Him out." But He has been trying to find us and reveal Himself to us. And the glory and the wonder of this makes us grateful beyond any other gratitude we could have. That He has gone so far to let us know of Him, what He is like, what He expects of us and what He is like toward us. That He has indeed translated Himself into the lauguage of a literal human life—a literal human life—Christ is one of us, blood of our blood, flesh of our flesh, bone of our bone who really lived in a real place, followed a real calling, had a real ministry with real people, one who really suffered, really died, really triumphed over death. And all this we have before us as the vivid expression of meaning. This is what saves us from mere intellectual abstraction. This is what saves us from relying upon just some logic or some hope. Jesus Christ is one you can see, you can read about in God's Holy Word, you can experience in the body of Christ as a living witness in the world even now two thousand years later; indeed, the body of Christ—His arms, His eyes, His ears—His "members" literally are acting for Him in the world as we can see the power of that action—we can actually gather together in the breaking of the bread and He is made known to us as always. So, there it is, a meaning that does make more sense out of the whole of life than any competing meaning. The only religion in the world which has claimed that God Himself has come among us that we might have the meanings, that we might know how to live, that we might know how we can be related to the Ultimate Ground of the universe, to the purpose of being.

A word about whether we need a meaning or not. There are many who seem very comfortable without God. But they aren't really fulfilled as persons. And that's very simple. Why? Because that's what they were made to be. Now, we are not made to function fully without being "plugged in." The way we are made is such that we are fulfilled only when we're in touch with the power of the living God. When we're not "plugged in," we can move along sometimes and do pretty well—I know that—during a great many years of my life when I was agnostic, I managed pretty well; but the fullness, the richness, the confidence, the courage and the power of living came to me when I began to function, at least a bit, the way I was made to function, which was with God. St. Augustine put it somewhat more eloquently in his famous words, "Thou, O Lord, hast formed us for thyself and our souls are restless until they find their rest in thee." We are not complete until we have found this meaning of life. "In the beginning was the Word, and the Word was with God, and the Word was God. . . . All things were made through him. . . . In him was life; and the life was the light of men. . . . The true Light that enlightens every man was coming into the world. . . . But to all who received him, who believed in his name, he gave power to become children of God. . . . And the Word became flesh and dwelt among us, full of grace and truth; we have beheld his glory, glory as of the only Son from the Father." AMEN.

"This Generation Will Not Pass Away . . ."

by Schubert M. Ogden *

(Scripture: " 'And there will be signs in sun and moon and stars, and upon the earth distress of nations in perplexity at the roaring of the sea and the waves, men fainting with fear and with foreboding of what is coming on the world; for the powers of the heavens will be shaken. And then they will see the Son of Man coming in a cloud with power and great glory. Now when these things begin to take place, look up and raise your heads, because your redemption is drawing near.' And he told them a parable: 'Look at the fig tree, and all the trees; as soon as they come out in leaf, you see for yourselves and know that the summer is already near. So also, when you see these things taking place, you know that the kingdom of God is near. Truly, I say to you, this generation will not pass away till all has taken place. Heaven and earth will pass away but my words will not pass away. But take heed to yourselves lest your hearts be weighed down with dissipation and drunkenness and cares of this life, and

* Schubert M. Ogden is Associate Professor in Perkins School of Theology, Southern Methodist University. This sermon was preached at Rockefeller Chapel, University of Chicago.

123

that day come upon you suddenly like a snare; for it will come upon all who dwell upon the face of the whole earth. But watch at all times, praying that you may have strength to escape all these things that will take place, and to stand before the Son of Man.'" Luke 21:25–36)

I

One of the great texts in the church's lectionary is the Gospel appointed for today, the Second Sunday in Advent. For generations, the church has made use of this text to proclaim its message of the coming of God's kingdom of judgment and grace. Nor can there be any question that the church intends the lesson also for us. Its message is addressed not only to this man or that man, but to all men— and this means also to you and me.

There is a question, however, whether this lesson can any longer communicate the church's message to us today. Intended for us it may be, but if we are to be confronted with the Word it speaks, it must be a lesson that we can understand. Yet this is the very thing we cannot take for granted. Neither for us nor for our contemporaries generally is it self-evident that this lesson has anything to say to us at all. There is a twofold reason for this.

First, the lesson, like so much of the New Testament writings, presupposes a mythological picture of the world. By "mythological" here I mean what is commonly understood by the word as it is used in the scientific study of religions—namely, a kind of view in which the realm of the transcendent, of the holy or the divine, is naïvely pictured in the terms and concepts that properly apply only to the created order. Thus, for example, the mythological mind typically thinks of God as dwelling in a heavenly world only spatially distant from the world of ordinary events and experiences. So in our text Jesus obviously imagines just this when he pictures the Son of Man descending on the clouds of heaven with power and great glory and exhorts his hearers to look up and raise their heads when these events of the end begin to take place. Likewise, his statements that redemption (or the kingdom of God) is "drawing near" suggest that he thinks as naïvely of the divine realm in terms of time as in terms of space. The future advent of God's kingdom is but one more event—although, of course, a miraculous one—in the midst and alongside of the other events in the historical process.

Therefore, from the standpoint of the student of religions, what is reflected in our text is simply the mythological world-picture of late Jewish apocalypticism that was so prominent a feature of the environment in which Christianity took its rise. With its expectation of the imminent end of the age and its ample inventory of the stock features of apocalyptic fantasy, the passage is a typical instance of the mythological view of the world everywhere presupposed in the earliest expressions of the Christian message.

But, second, such a mythological view is bound to seem alien and incredible to us today. As a result of the phenomenal development of science and technology, which is the most significant happening in the modern history of the West, our thinking has been so determined that the mytho-

logical world-picture of the Christian tradition cannot but
strike us as irrevocably passé. Nor is this true only of those
of us who directly share in the ongoing processes of scientific
research and are sophisticated about scientific thinking and
procedure. Even the ordinary man in the street, whose view
of the world is increasingly determined by the achievements
of technology, is unable to credit traditional mythological
claims. He knows as surely as the trained scientist how sense-
less it is to speak of "up" and "down" in the universe in
which he lives, and how impossible, therefore, is the notion
of a heavenly realm situated somewhere "above" the world
of mundane occurrences. And if the astronomer, as Laplace
said, has no need of the "God hypothesis" to account for
the movements of the stars, the common man has just as
little need of it to make use of his electric shaver or the
countless other appliances of a technological civilization.

Furthermore, man today cannot honestly look forward
to the imminent or eventual end of the world and Christ's
coming on the clouds of heaven to hold judgment and to
dispense supernatural salvation and damnation. He is ac-
customed to view the course of events as an immensely
intricate natural process that follows its own orderly laws
of change and development, and if he even thinks of the
world's coming to an end, he takes for granted that this,
too, would be due to natural and not supernatural causes
or conditions.

To be sure, the dreaded prospect of thermonuclear annihilation sometimes seems to give the terrors of the apocalypse
a meaning for us they scarcely had a generation ago. But

anyone who thinks about it realizes that the destruction of our earth in a nuclear holocaust is something completely different from an end of the world brought about by the intervention of divine or supernatural powers. And when confronted with Jesus' words that "this generation will not pass away till all has taken place," the contemporary man is bound to ask whether the refutation of this promise by over nineteen hundred years of history is not more than sufficient evidence of its illusiveness.

No one will question, of course, that there are exceptions to this generalization and that superstition in various forms continues to manifest itself on the edges of our scientific civilization. Even so, the real exceptions are probably far fewer than we might suppose were we to judge solely from what men profess to believe. Do we not often protest our assent to things that in fact have little or no bearing on the way we understand our lives? And what of the different forms of superstition that we see? Do they not confirm the generalization rather than deny it? Are not the credulous souls who crowd around the astrology counter in the downtown five-and-dime store in a very different position from the devout believers in astral religion who were so numerous a company in late antiquity?

The superstitious man of today stands at the periphery and not at the center of his civilization; and it is obvious— at times, surely, even to him—that he is fighting a losing battle. At any rate, those of us who are gathered here, like the vast majority of our contemporaries, cannot accept as our own the mythological picture of the world reflected in our text. Because we are the modern men we are, we must ask not only what it is this text would say to us, but whether it has anything to say to us at all. Is there any way of interpreting it that will permit it to say all it really intends to to say, and yet do this so that we today who no longer think mythologically can understand it as confronting us with a genuine possibility of decision?

II

There is a way of approaching our text that permits it to speak to us, and if we follow this way it will be discovered to have something to say to us that we desperately need to hear. In any event, it will be seen to offer us a possibility for understanding our lives that confronts us with a real choice. If we are unable to make this choice and to understand ourselves as it directs, this will not be because it asks us to believe an incredible mythology, but because we are unwilling to make the kind of personal decision it summons us to make.

The clue to our text's meaning is to recognize that the real purpose of its mythological language is only very imperfectly achieved by this language itself. The intention of myth is to speak of the transcendent reality that we experience as the ground and limit of our own existence and of the entire created order. In speaking of this reality, however, myth so represents it that it seems to be just one more item in the cosmic whole. Thus myth appears as though its purpose is scientific rather than religious, as though it is another way of knowing about the same reality that the various sciences properly know. As a result, it seems to conflict with the sciences insofar as they refuse to credit the claims it apparently makes.

But this conflict completely obscures myth's real intention; and this is true even though the language of myth makes the conflict seem plausible and the partisans of myth are often tragically slow in recognizing its real purpose. Myth does not really intend to speak about matters that are the proper concern of the special sciences, but rather seeks to express our inalienable sense of dependence upon an ultimate source of being and meaning, which is the ever-present ground of all created things.

Thus the purpose of apocalyptic mythology in speaking about the end of the world is not to provide a bizarre description of extraordinary phenomena, but rather to present an understanding of human life that is a perennial possibility for our decision. It wants to say that the final justification for our lives and for the whole created order is never to be found within that order itself, but solely in the grace and judgment of God that constantly impinge on us as our final end. What alone endows our lives with abiding importance is that they make a difference to something beyond themselves—not simply that they give rise to other created events that must also cry out for justification, but that the whole creative process at each of its stages is assessed by a transcendent judgment and thereby rendered everlastingly significant.

Apart from such a judgment, for which nothing that happens is merely indifferent and which is able to preserve the present from perishing into the past, our creaturely lives would be utterly devoid of meaning. For mortal men like us, the rule holds fast that "in the midst of life we are in death." Nor is this merely the death that must one day bring each of our lives to its close. It is also the deeper death whereby every present accomplishment is "perpetually perishing." Hardly have we grasped the present and made it ours than it slips away forever into the receding past. Our poor powers of memory and judgment are unable to retain it in the living immediacy of the new present; and if it lingers with us at all, it is as but a shade of its former reality.

Hence our deep need to be accepted, to be known and cherished for exactly what we are, can never be met by the judgments of men. Although we seek one another's approval, and despair when we do not find it, we are haunted by the knowledge that the final judgment for which we yearn, the ultimate acceptance that can alone endow our lives with meaning, cannot be supplied us by creatures like ourselves.

It is of just such a final judgment, however, that apocalyptic mythology intends to speak. Its purpose is not to refer us to some incredible happening in the near or remote future, but rather to point us to the transcendent love of God that hovers over every happening as its ultimate end. In this way, it summons us to a new understanding of our lives. It tells us that we both can and should understand ourselves in the light of God's love and so realize the inner freedom from our past and for our future that his love makes possible.

When our text, then, speaks of the dramatic events that will signal the end of the present age and the imminent coming of the Son of Man to bring final judgment and redemption, it is really speaking of the two most insistent realities of our human condition. It reminds us that in the world in which we live nothing whatever is fixed and permanent. So far as we can see, our lives and the whole created order to which we belong are constantly slipping into the nothingness of the past. And when it speaks of "distress of nations" and "men fainting with fear and with foreboding of what is coming on the world," it but expresses our anxiety when this transience of every creaturely present suddenly overwhelms us.

But it is in just this situation of anxiety, it says, that our redemption is "drawing near." The point is not that God is closer to us when we are anxious, or that the cracks in things more clearly reveal his presence than things themselves. Rather, it is the same point expressed in the old saying that "our extremity is God's opportunity." Just when we are overcome by the perpetual perishing of all our good and by our utter helplessness to secure for our lives any abiding meaning, we may be led to look up and raise our heads to receive the security of God's grace. In this sense, the passing away of the present order and the shaking of even the powers of the heavens are "signs" of God's approaching redemption. As surely as the leafing of the trees is followed by the coming of summer, so surely are the transient events of our lives followed by the advent of God's everlasting kingdom.

And most important, all this is happening now! "Truly, I say to you, this generation will not pass away"—will not slip forever from the immediacy of the present—"till all has taken place"—till it is completely known and loved in the final judgment of God. The ultimate end of every present, of this very moment now, is to be received into the everlasting kingdom of God's love and there to be known and cherished forever for exactly what it is. What for us constantly slips into the irrecoverable past is for God preserved in an eternal present from which nothing can ever be lost. And this eternal present of his love, of his judgment and grace, is even now the ultimate context in which all our lives are set.

Thus our text summons us to a new understanding of ourselves. Because the final truth about us is that even now we are all freely received by God's love, we are both enabled and commanded to be free from our past and open for the future. We need not and ought not to be burdened by the cares of this life, by the anxious striving to secure our existence in a perishing world. It is just when we lose ourselves in the things of the world by trying to find in them a meaning for our lives that we fall subject to the power of death. Then it is that the inevitable transience of the creature can come upon us suddenly like a snare. When we set our hearts too completely on the perishing goods of the present age and fail to remember the final shadow under which they all stand, we but make ourselves vulnerable to their inevitable passing away.

Therefore, our text admonishes us to be watchful at all times and to pray for the strength to escape from the fate of every created thing. It is not that we are to ask to be relieved of the necessity of dying, much less to be gathered to some heavenly realm where this necessity supposedly no longer exists. The fact is sure that both "heaven and earth will pass away" and that heaven will pass away no less completely than earth. No, the only strength for which we are to pray is the strength that comes from God's unending love; and the only escape we may rightly seek is the escape this love alone provides.

But with this strength we may also hope to stand before the Son of Man. In being freed from our past and the anxious care that binds us to it, we can and should be open to meet the needs of our neighbors. And, as we are taught by another word in the New Testament, to realize this possibility and fulfill this demand is precisely what it means to stand in the day of the Lord's appearing. "Then the King will say to those at his right hand, 'Come, O blessed of my Father, inherit the kingdom prepared for you from the foundation of the world; for . . . as you did it to one of the least of these my brethren, you did it to me' " (Matt. 25:34-40). In every encounter with our neighbor in which we are open to meet his needs, we receive nothing less than the final benediction of the Lord Christ himself; and in that day when he shall come in all his glory—which is to say, in the very moment of our present encounter—we shall surely be caused to stand.

This is the meaning our text has for us. And when we so interpret it, it teaches us to understand not only the significance of the season of Advent, but also the innermost meaning of the Christian message itself. For to live as a Christian means to have just this understanding of one's life—to look forward to the imminent coming of God's kingdom and thereby to be freed from one's past and open for the future, with its gift and demand.

To be sure, the Christian looks forward to this coming kingdom on the strength of a Word that has already come to him in the life and death of Jesus Christ. But this Word already spoken is a promise in time redeemed only in eternity. The kingdom of God to which it points is a kingdom that is always coming and only in this sense a kingdom that has already come. It impinges on every moment as its ultimate end and so is eternally present. But it is never present so that it may be simply identified with some particular happening or stage in the temporal order. Rather, as the decisive event of God's grace and judgment, it is always beyond the world and is also eternally future.

Thus it is that the Christian life is no merely static thing that may be settled once and for all by an act of intellectual assent to certain beliefs. It is not at all a matter of beliefs, whether mythological or not, but is entirely a matter of understanding one's own personal life, which must constantly be settled anew by the concrete decision of the moment.

MAY GOD give us the grace to make this decision and to keep ourselves open for the coming of his kingdom. For the promise of the text is sure: "This generation will not pass away till all has taken place." AMEN.

The Nature of Faith

by Ronald Gregor Smith *

(Scripture: "When they had preached the gospel to that
city and made many disciples, they returned to Lystra
and to Iconium and to Antioch, strengthening the souls
of the disciples, exhorting them to continue in the faith,
and saying that through many tribulations we must enter
the kingdom of God. And when they had appointed
elders for them in every church, with prayer and fasting,
they committed them to the Lord in whom they believed." Acts 14:21–23)

Many people seem to think that faith requires some special
talent or even special taste—similar to a liking for caviar or
for the music of Beethoven. Or they think that faith is some
kind of trick which is really an illegitimate attempt to find a
short cut through an impassable jungle. But I think that the
commonest complication among such sophisticated people
as yourselves is that faith is regarded as just one more among
the burdens which you are required to carry if you want to

* Ronald Gregor Smith was formerly editor of the Student Christian
Movement Press and is now Professor at the University of Glasgow. This
message was given at the British S.C.M. Conference in 1961.

be a Christian. You are required to love everybody. You are required to be amiable and optimistic—and, in general, ever more and more of a paragon. And then, on top of all this, you are required to have faith: faith is the special burden laid on top of all the others. No wonder it often becomes the last straw that breaks the camel's back!

Against all this I should say that there is an ultimate simplicity in faith. And I think that anyone with some experience of the world beyond the twilight world of the universities, where ideas so easily become specters and incubi, could agree that there are in fact people everywhere, ordinary people, whose life is quite transparent: they are simply living in faith.

I do not want to forget these people as I launch out with you now. I much hope that when we have come through—whether "through" means just this hour, or who knows what days or years of struggle—we shall also reach that kind of simplicity in our faith.

But just because we have entered the world of ideas, and their history and interaction, and the world of self-conscious appraisal, we have left that world of simple faith behind us. And all around us, and in us, there are other worlds—and in particular the world without faith, the secular, the world which gets along perfectly well without God, which manages its own affairs better or worse on its own responsibility, and which, even if it manages them worse and worse, is still unable to find any other help, or any other way, than just how it has begun: without reference to God.

I think that there is a real connection between Christian

faith and this independence of the world. I think that it is a proper consequence of a properly held Christian faith that there should be this autonomy and freedom of the world to go its own way—even if this freedom involves, again and again, a departure from the very ground of faith.

But I can explain what I mean by this only after I have tried to get at this ground of faith. You may have noticed that I have already quietly slipped in the word "Christian." I think the word "faith" can be used in other contexts. For instance, we can legitimately say that we believe in so-and-so, or that a physicist believes in the regularity of nature when he makes, or repeats, an experiment. And I should not wish to deprive adherents of other religions of the use of this word "to believe," "to have faith." But not only in our own historical context, but also in the nature of the thing, Christian faith is faith *par excellence*. It is not an accident, or a sign of mere intolerance, that quite early in the history of Christianity, even in the letters of Paul and quite clearly in the Acts of the Apostles, the word "faith" is used absolutely of Christian faith. Stephen is called "a man full of faith" (Acts 6:5) and Paul on his journeys is described as exhorting the new disciples "to continue in the faith" (Acts 14:22).

If I now ask, what does this summary word mean, precisely, then the provisional answer can only be that faith is coterminous with all that Christianity is. Then the questions rise thick and fast: Are we talking about something that goes on in you, or something that comes to you from outside yourself? Is this faith something *by* which you believe, something *in* which you believe, or simply *which* you believe? Is it a state of your soul or, at the other extreme, is it a body of teaching, doctrines, dogma, to which you subscribe? Is it an addition to the things you can learn about the world and God by your unaided reason? And if it is such an addition, is it a completion or fulfillment of these thing, or does it go against them, so that it must simply be called an irrational thing? In what sense are the notorious words to be taken which the early thinker Tertullian is alleged to have spoken, *credo quia absurdum* ("I believe because it is absurd")? Are we really talking of something which passes comprehension? Or if there is a paradox here, can it be sustained and not simply written off as a logical contradiction?

There are more refined questions still. For instance, can faith be fully described in psychological terms and so reduced to an anthropology? Is faith inevitably bound up with a specific metaphysic, especially the medieval view of a compound structure of being, the realm of the natural and the realm of the supernatural—which you must first accept if you are to find a place for faith?

Questions of this kind have their due place in a study of faith because of a prior fact about faith. It is this: Faith is essentially historical. It arises as a consequence of certain events in history, and at the same time these historical events constitute its content. To put it in more particular and positive terms, faith—to borrow a definition from Rudolf Bultmann—is the "obedient submission to God's revelation in the word of proclamation." To put it still more strictly, this proclaimed Word, which we find at the very heart of the

Christian events, is the Word through Christ of God's forgiveness of our sins. This Word is not simply a statement,
which can then be set down along with other propositions,
which we have then to subscribe to. But it is a Word which
is lived: it is an historical action, given in a revelatory event,
namely, the event of the life and death of Jesus. Faith, which
is submission to this event, is likewise an action. It is a free
decision on your part, in the totality of your historical being.
But just because it is a decision of yours when faced with
the question which is put to you in this lived Word, Jesus,
by God, this decision is at the same time and in the same
action something done to you. The faith is yours, but it is
also created in you. It takes its shape in your life in ac-
cordance with the content which it already has as the historical Word of God. So to live *in faith* is to live *by* that
historical Word which both demands your response and
effects upon you God's liberating forgiveness. Faith may
therefore now be defined as the free response to the forgiving
Word of God, which frees us to live in the world for God's
future.

If you ask, how can we call our response a free response
if it is the forgiving Word which sets us free, then I can
only point to our actual historical situation. We are free to
decide, for or against this Word. If we decide for it, then our
life is qualified and determined henceforth by this free decision. Your life will never be the same again. It is henceforth
qualified by the historical Word of God. And this means
that a shift has taken place in the totality of your being. You
recognize and acknowledge, simultaneously with your own

responsibility, your utter dependence upon God. But this does not eliminate your freedom. It sets you on a new way. This new way is not out of your world. But you are, as it were, taken out of your world by this free response and then put back in it again. Nothing less than the totality of your historical existence is at stake. But this historical existence of yours is not destroyed. Nor is it just veneered over with a gloss of mystical feelings. Nor is some quality just added to your life, a strange something called grace poured into your soul. But you have made a decision, in relation to a constellation of historical events, by which henceforth you are ready to live your life. You are not given something which you henceforth possess, either in the form of a new inward experience or in the form of a series of doctrines, but you are set in a new relation to yourself and to your world, by God.

Now, it is clear that the descriptions which faith gives of itself through history do in fact change. Faith seeks to understands itself, and seeks to express itself, in the changing circumstances of history. And so it is not surprising that it should appear differently at different times. It can even misunderstand itself—and if does this long enough then it can lose itself and turn into something else. But it is also true that unless faith is constantly understanding itself anew in new circumstances, it will not be true to itself. For the free decision of faith has to be constantly renewed, and in face of its own doubts, in face of its constant, varying temptations, and in face of the ever new opportunities which it has of being tested against the questions and demands of the world.

I want to take two examples of the self-understanding of

faith, one traditional and one modern, by which we can throw the basic matter into relief. The first, traditional view is the medieval scholastic view of faith as consisting of three distinct parts which follow in chronological sequence. The first element is that of *notitia,* or knowledge. The second is *assensus,* or assent. And the third is *fiducia,* or trust. First you get knowledge, then you give your assent to it, and finally you trust in it. Now, it is easy to be impatient with this kind of formal analysis; and I myself am prepared to criticize it quite severely. But the point of the criticism I should make is not that the scholastic thinkers desired the reasonableness of faith, which remained reasonable even in the ultimate analysis, in the sense that though faith in the end passed beyond the scope of the natural reason, it was never *irrational.* For I think that Christian faith is not simply to be charged with being irrational or merely arbitrary. My point of criticism of this threefold distinction is rather the assumption which lies behind it. It is that the faith which we are called to accept is capable of being described in a series of propositions, or in a collection of pieces of information, such as you find put down in the creeds of the church, or in the minutes of the ecumenical councils. The *notitia* or knowledge which is the first stage in the acceptance of faith is a series of assertions which have behind them the authority of the church. This authority is certainly derived from the authoritative revelation. But the revelation itself is regarded as a pronouncement, or a series of pronouncements, about the being of God and the life of man. The power of faith is therefore narrowed to the one deep but strange channel of what is basically a collection of arbitrary messages, which you are authoritatively asked to accept. In effect, the authority is the authority of man. It is the claim which logically ends in the claim to infallibility made by an historical institution. It doesn't matter whether at this point your obedience is to the Pope or to the Bible—the latter in the sense of the familiar children's hymn, "Jesus loves me, this I know, for the Bible tells me so." Neither authority can claim the real obedience of faith. The only claimant is God in his Word, and by his Word; once again, I mean the liberating Word of forgiveness in Christ.

Here then we see, in this traditional analysis, an understanding of faith which tries to evade the ground of faith. The ground is the living historical Word.

Now take the modern example. Here the difficulty in the traditional view is met by an extreme view which is also, in my mind, unacceptable. This modern view is very clear that faith is not to be equated with knowledge by inference and argument. You cannot express God. You can only address him. Knowledge by acquaintance is replaced by direct knowledge. The whole emphasis is laid upon trust, upon knowing God as you know another person. The I meets the Thou. It is not the God of the philosophers, the God of ideas, the God who is no more than an idea, but the living God, the God of Abraham, who is the partner in a living faith. You meet him in a direct encounter. There is a personal presence, in which you speak not of "knowing about" but simply knowing. Here faith is equated with trust: you trust in the living God, who is entirely self-authenticating in the actual moment of encounter.

Now far be it from me to wish to throw overboard the insights which have been regained for Christendom, especially by the writings of Martin Buber, with whose thought I have had so much to do, and who is the leading spirit behind all this way of thinking. If we call it personalism, and so try to classify it, we must never forget that in an irreducible way the Christian does encounter in his faith a God who, whatever else he is, is also in some sense personal.

But what I should say is that this kind of personalist equation of faith with a directness or immediacy of meeting with God does not do justice to the historicity of faith. Faith—let me repeat—is obedient submission to God's revelation in the Word of the *kerygma* or proclamation. If you wish to sum it up in the word "trust"—as I think you can—then you must always add that it is trust in one who is trustworthy, who has disclosed himself as trustworthy. And with this addition you are thrown back into the historical situation, back to the events recorded in the Bible, and back to the whole ambiguous history of Christianity—ambiguous in the past, and ambiguous in your present life. You cannot halt at the immediacy of an encounter and say that here is the ultimate simplicity of faith. For, once again, faith arises in virtue of certain historical events, events which themselves shape the faith which you enter upon. I do not think that Martin Buber is either a mystic or a pantheist or that his account of faith is merely subjective. But I do think that he abstracts faith from its historical situation. So much of what he says is right and valuable and needs to be said! What he does not say is absolutely cardinal: that in Christ we have the historical offer of a faith which binds us both to our history and to God.

With these two examples in our mind, we can move to some kind of conclusion. It should be clear enough that faith is not something you possess, but a relation into which you enter. It is also clear that though faith is ineluctably historical, in its origin and in its unfolding, it is not something that you can simply inherit from your father or from your teachers or by any other claim upon a tradition. The tradition is dormant until you have made your own decision and so entered upon the inheritance.

Relation

Two other things must be mentioned. First, the question of paradox; second, the question of secularism.

Paradox—I can put this vast matter quite briefly: For Christian faith there is only one paradox, that is the forgiving action of God in Christ. This is not irrational or absurd. You know very well what forgiveness is. What Christian faith responds to is the proclaiming of forgiveness by God in Christ in his life and his death. This is not a logical contradiction at all. But it is the unheard-of, unimaginable entry of God into human life in his absolute being for men. I shall not go into the intricate and fascinating work of modern New Testament scholars who have tried with more or less success to keep this insight free of the encumbrances of tradition and of inevitable error. All I shall say is that this single paradox is entirely grounded in Christ: He is the ground of our faith. He who was in his life the witness of faith has become through His absolute being for others the ground and basis of faith. Christ is not simply God. But He is the Word of God, entered into human being, and freeing us for a life of love, in faith.

I cannot give you any grounds for this faith, external to this one ground, Christ himself. He is the beginning of the way of faith, and He is also the end.

But the end is not yet. We can rightly say that the end is anticipated in faith. In a fundamental sense we have already passed in faith beyond even the last trial of faith, which is death. It is all over, and we live in faith as though nothing mattered. But we are not indifferent. For faith casts us back into the world.

And this brings me to my last point: secularism. I said earlier that there is a real connection between Christian faith and the independence of the world. The independence of the world is a contemporary fact. We could all give innumerable examples of how men live their lives today without reference to God. And indeed, this is not a new phenomenon. We are living today at the end of an age which began with immense hopes and an immense sense of liberation from outmoded forms of belief. What is the significance of this? It is not possible to say that it is either a mere rebellion against God or a simple necessity of historical development. History remains ambiguous and a mystery till the end. None of us can see the whole meaning of it. But what we can say derives from the nature of the Christian faith. The description of faith which I have given you involves man's freedom to decide. And with his decision for faith, as it has been made in the historical past, one of the accompaniments was the liberation of the world. Man recognized his responsibility for his own history. The world was no longer a mythological theater for the battle between good and evil spirits. The world of *Gnosis,* and the world of mythology, were exorcized. The world became man's, in faith. It was not merely demythologized: it was dedivinized. Man became the decider of his own future. He was liberated from magic spells and from incomprehensible authority.

All this was implicit in the free acceptance of the Word from God, freeing man from anxiety about himself and the world. God's action in Christ was a separation as well as an advent. The fact that his Word comes contains the faith that He is also not of this world. Men are now invited to be heirs, to grow up, and to accept their responsibility for the world. For Christian faith takes you right into history, and it makes you responsible for history, as the place where God is. But God is not in the historical world as a part of the world; nor is he, on the other hand, merely cut off from the world. It is here, in the heart of Christian faith, that the ambiguity of history is found at its most potent. For faith affirms the presence of God in history which at its climax is simultaneously an absence of God. This is the special dialectic of faith, which it encounters in the historical situation, in the Word made flesh, the conjoined presence and absence of God. This is the nearest to directness which you can get in Christianity, and its qualifying term is always faith: we believe in God through Christ. This is what Dietrich Bonhoeffer means, in that strange sentence in one of his letters, when he says, "God teaches us to live in the world without God." This intense dialectic is sustained at the very center of Christianity as its proper scandal or stumbling block; and the only way of sustaining it is faith.

In view of all this, it is not surprising that you should find today, in spite of every anxiety, a tremendous exhilaration in the powers of man. For these powers are no longer infected by the ancient fears of devils or angels. They are rightly regarded as powers which are part of man's self-responsibility. Christian faith recognizes them as powers of freedom, which are intrinsic to the givenness of all men's gifts. The Christian believer is captivated by the mystery of the existence of the world and his own existence. (He is an ontologist at heart: he cannot think the idea of God without knowing the Presence.) It is the Christian's duty—or rather he cannot avoid believing, that in this free responsibility which he has, the element of givenness runs through everything: through his hopes and enterprises, through his fears and doubts, and through his inklings of glory. This givenness is the ground of his hope: the givenness of history, and especially of the phenomenon of Jesus as the Word. This hope can be expressed in many different ways, and has in fact, like faith, taken a great variety of forms in the course of history. And in our own time, in which secularism is the form into which everything turns—in van Peursen's words, "there are no more transcendental things but just worldly things"—then are we not left with a completely intramundane and functional world? Has the secularist movement not led us to mere relativism in all our judgments? Again, I say, hope takes many forms. And the form which it can take today, as I think, is one in which the autonomy of this world is still sustained by the tension which may issue in a new theonomy —God not *in* the world, nor *over* the world as a metaphysical substance, but through Christ in the world, present to faith.

I have said the Christian faith is not irrational. At the same time, there is no limit set. The Christian believes that in Christ everything is reconciled to God. For we believe that Christ is the perfecter as well as the pioneer of our faith. So we believe that a time like the present, which is full of anxiety about the future of history, is a time in which faith may come into its own. Faith too has a future: God's future. And in this ultimate recourse there is a kind of certainty: the certainty of a personal and fighting faith.

Spiritual Presence

by Paul Tillich *

(Scripture: Joel 2:28–29; Ezek. 36:22–28; Rom. 8:12–17;
I Cor. 2:9–15.

"Not that we are sufficient of ourselves to claim anything as coming from us; our sufficiency is from God,
who has qualified us to be ministers of a new covenant,
not in a written code but in the Spirit; for the written
code kills, but the Spirit gives life." II Cor. 3:5–6)

I

"Not that we are sufficient"—writes Paul. Who are the
"we"? Obviously, the apostle himself and those who work
with him. This includes all those who are qualified to serve
the "new covenent," as he calls it, namely the new relationship between God and man, and through it the "new creation," the new state of things in man and his world, of
which Paul is a messenger. And qualified to serve is everyone who himself participates in it, however fragmentarily.
But if we ask, who *does* participate in the new creation, then

* Paul Tillich is Professor Emeritus in Union Theological Seminary
and former University Professor at Harvard University.

149

we soon find this to be a question without answer. For nobody can look into the innermost center of any other being, not even fully into his own heart. Therefore, nobody can say with certainty that anyone else shares in the new state of things; he can scarcely say it of himself. Even less can he say of another one, however distorted this man's life may be, that he does not participate at all in the new reality, and that he is not qualified at all to serve its cause. And, certainly, nobody can say this of himself.

Perhaps it is more important in our time to emphasize the latter, namely, the qualification of ourselves and those around us to serve the new creation, our ability to be priests in mutual help toward achieving it. Not long ago many people, especially members of the churches, felt qualified to judge others and to tell them what to believe and how to act. Today we feel deeply the arrogance of this attitude. Instead of that a general awareness of our lack of qualification is everywhere manifest, especially in the middle-aged and younger generations. We are inclined to disqualify ourselves and to withdraw from the service of the new creation. We feel that we don't participate in it and that we cannot bring others into such participation. We decline the honor and the burden of mutual priesthood. Often this is caused by unconcern for our highest human vocation; but equally it is caused by despair about ourselves, by doubt, guilt and emptiness. We feel infinitely removed from a new state of things and totally unable to help others toward it.

But then the other words of our text must become effective, that our qualification is from God and not from our-

selves; and the all-consoling word that God is greater than
our heart. If we look beyond ourselves at that which is
greater than we, then we can feel called to help others just
in a moment in which we ourselves need help most urgently
—and astonishingly, we *can* help. A power works through
us which is not from us. Perhaps we remember a situation in
which words came out of the depth of our being, maybe in
a state of our own great anxiety, which hit another one in
the depth of *his* being and *his* state of great anxiety so
strongly that they helped him to a new state of things. Perhaps we remember another situation in which an action of a
person whose disrupted life we knew had a priestly, awakening, healing effect upon us. It came not from him, but it was
in him, as on the other occasion it came not from us, but
was in us. Let us not assume the task of being mediators
of the new creation to others arrogantly, be it in personal or
in ecclesiastical arrogance. Yet, let us not reject the task of
being priest for each other because of desperation about ourselves or in unconcern about what should be our highest
concern. Against both arrogance and despair stands the
word that our qualification does not come from us, nor from
any man or any institution, not even from a church, but
from God. And if it comes from God, it is his Spiritual
Presence in our spirit.

II

When we now hear the word "Spirit," we are somehow
prepared for it: the power in us, but not from us, qualifying
us for the service of a new state of things, that is what Spirit

means. This may sound strange to the many inside and out-side the churches for whom the term Holy Spirit is the strangest of the strange terms which appear in the world of Christian symbols. Rarely a subject of preaching, it is also neglected in religious teaching. Its festival, Pentecost, has almost disappeared in the popular consciousness of this country. Some groups which claim spiritual experiences of a particular character are considered unhealthy—and rightly so. Liturgically, the use of the term "Holy Ghost" produces an impression of great remoteness from our way of speaking and thinking. But spiritual experience is a reality in every-one, as solid as the experience of being loved or the experi-ence of the air one breathes. Therefore, we should not shy away from the word "Spirit." We should become fully aware of the Spiritual Presence, around us and in us, even if we realize how limited may be our experience of "God present to our spirit." For this is what Divine Spirit means: God present to our spirit. Spirit is not a mysterious sub-stance, it is not a part of God; it is God himself; but not God as the creative ground of all things and not God as directing history and manifesting himself in its central event, but God is present in communities and personalities, grasp-ing them, inspiring them, transforming them.

For Spirit is first of all power, the power which drives the human spirit above itself toward what it cannot attain by itself: the love which is greater than all other gifts, the truth in which the depth of being opens itself to us, the Holy which is the manifestation of the presence of the ultimate.

You may say again: "I do not know this power, I never

had such an experience. I am not religious or, at least, not a Christian and certainly not a bearer of the Spirit. What I heard from you sounded like ecstasy; and I want to stay sober; it sounded like mystery, and I try to illuminate what is dark; it sounded like self-sacrifice and I want to fulfill my human possibilities." To this I answer: Certainly, the Spiritual Power can drive some people into an ecstasy which most of us have never experienced, it can drive some toward a kind of self-sacrifice of which most of us are not capable, it can drive some to insights into the depth of being which remain unapproachable to most of us. But this does not justify our denial that the Spirit is also working in us. Without doubt, wherever it works, there is an element, possibly very small, of self-surrender, and an element, however weak, of ecstasy, and an element, perhaps fleeting, of awareness of the mystery of existence. Yet these small effects of the Spiritual Power are enough to prove its presence.

But there are other conscious and noticeable manifestations of the Spiritual Presence. Let me enumerate some of them, while you may ask yourselves whether and to what degree they are your own experiences. The Spirit can work in you with a soft but insistent voice, telling you that your life is empty and meaningless, but that there are chances of a new life waiting before the door of your inner self to fill its void and to conquer its dullness. The Spirit can work in you, awakening the desire to strive toward the sublime over against the profanity of the average day. The Spirit can give you the courage which says "yes" to life in spite of the destructiveness you have experienced around you and within you. The Spirit can reveal to you that you have hurt somebody deeply, but it also can give you the right word which reunites him with you. The Spirit can make you love with the divine love someone you profoundly dislike or hate or who has no interest for you. The Spirit can conquer the laziness toward what you know is the aim of your life, and it can change your bad, aggressive and depressed mood into stability and serenity.

The Spirit can liberate you from hidden enmity against those whom you love and from open revengefulness against those by whom you feel violated. The Spirit can give you the strength to throw away false anxieties and to take upon yourself the anxiety which belongs to life itself. The Spirit can awaken you to sudden insight into the way you must take, and it can open your eyes to a view of your world which makes everything new. The Spirit can give you joy in the midst of the ordinary routine as well as in the depth of sorrow.

The Spirit can create warmth in the coldness you feel within you and around you, and it can give you wisdom and strength where your human love toward a loved one has failed. The Spirit can throw you into the hell of despair about yourself and then give you the certainty that life has accepted you just when you felt totally rejected, and when you rejected yourself totally. The Spirit can give you the power of prayer, which nobody has except through the Spiritual Presence. For every prayer—be it with or without words—that reaches its aim, namely, the reunion with the divine ground of our being, is a work of the Spirit speaking in us and through us. Prayer is a spiritual sighing and long-ing of a finite being to return to its origin.

These are works of the Spirit, signs of the Spiritual Pres-ence with us and in us. In view of these manifestations, who can assert that he is without Spirit? Who can say that he is in no way a bearer of the Spirit? He may be it in a small way; but is there anybody amongst us who could say more than that about himself?

One can compare the Spiritual Presence with the air we breathe, which surrounds us, is nearest to us, and works life within us. This comparison has a deep justification: in most languages, the word "spirit" means breath or wind. Some-times the wind becomes storm, grand and devastating; but mostly it is moving air, always present, not always noticed. In the same way the Spirit is always present, a moving power, sometimes in stormy ecstasies of individuals and groups, mostly quietly entering our human spirit and keep-ing it alive; sometimes manifest in great moments of his-tory or of a personal life, mostly working hiddenly through the media of our daily encounters with men and world; sometimes using its creation, the religious communities and their spiritual means, often making itself felt in spheres far removed from what is usually called religious. Like the wind, the Spirit blows where it wills! It is not subject to a rule or limited by a method. Its ways with men are not de-pendent on what men are and do. You cannot force the Spirit upon you, upon an individual, upon a group, not even upon a Christian church. Although He who is the founda-tion of the churches was Himself by the Spirit, and although

the Spirit as it was present in Him is the greatest manifestation of Spiritual Presence—the Spirit is not bound to the
Christian churches or any one of them. The Spirit is free to
work in the spirits of men in every human situation, and it
urges man to let him do so; God as Spirit is always present
to the spirit of man.

But why does the psalmist pray: "Take not thy Spirit
from me!" And why do we speak today of the "absent God,"
a term which plays a role in literature and art, and most of
all in the personal experience of innumerable people? How
can we unite the message of the Spiritual Presence with the
experience of the absent God? Let me say something of the
"absent God," asking, what is the cause of his absence? We
may answer: our resistance, our indifference, our lack of
seriousness, our honest or dishonest questioning, our genuine or cynical doubt! All these answers have some truth; but
they have not the last truth. The final answer to the question
who makes God absent, is God himself!

It is the work of the Spirit that removes God from our
sight, not only for some men, but sometimes for many in a
particular period. We live in an era in which the God we
know is the absent God. But in knowing God as the absent
God, we *know* of Him; we feel His absence as the empty
space which is left by something or someone which belonged
to us and has vanished from our view. God is always infinitely near and infinitely far. We are fully aware of Him
only if we experience both. But sometimes, when our awareness of Him has become shallow, habitual, not warm and
not cold, when He has become too familiar to be exciting,

too near to be felt in His infinite distance—then He becomes
the absent God. The Spirit has not ceased to be present. The
Spiritual Presence can never end. But the Spirit of God hides
God to our sight. No resistance against the Spirit, no indifference, no doubt can drive the Spirit away. But the Spirit
which always remains present to us can hide itself and that
means it can hide God. Then the Spirit shows us nothing except the absent God and the empty space within us which is
His space. The Spirit has shown to our time and to innumerable people in our time the absent God and the empty
space which cries in us to be filled by Him. And then the
absent one may return and take the space which belongs to
Him, and the Spiritual Presence may break again into our
consciousness, awakening us to recognize what we are,
shaking and transforming us. This may happen like the
coming of a storm, the storm of the Spirit, stirring up the
stagnant air of our spiritual life. The storm will recede, a
new stagnancy may take place, and the awareness of the
present God may be replaced by the awareness of its empty
space in us. Life in the Spirit is this up-and-down. And this
means: Whether we experience the present or the absent
God—it is a work of the Spirit.

III

And now let me describe a symptom of the Spiritual
Presence in us, the greatest of all, powerfully expressed in
Paul's words: "Not in written code, but in Spirit; for the
written code kills, but the Spirit gives life." This means that
the work of the Spiritual Presence in a man reaches its

height when it liberates from the yoke of the Commandments to the freedom of the Spirit. This is like releasing from the sentence of death to a new life. A tremendous experience lies behind these words, an experience in which we all can share, although it is rare in its full depth and is then a revolutionary power which through men like Paul and Augustine and Luther has changed the spiritual world and through it the history of mankind. Can we, you and I, share in this experience?

First, have we felt the deadening power of the written code, written not only in the Ten Commandments and their many interpretations in Bible and history, but also written with the pen of the authority of parents and society into the unconscious depths of our being, recognized by our conscience, judging us in what we do and, above all, in what we are? Nobody can flee from the voice of this written code, written internally as well as externally. And if we try to silence it, to close our ears against it, the Spirit itself frustrates these attempts, opening our ears toward the cries of our true being of that which we are and ought to be in the sight of eternity. We cannot escape this judgment against us. The Spirit itself, using the written code, makes this impossible. For the Spirit does not give life without having led us through the experience of death. And certainly the written code in its threatening majesty has the power to kill. It kills the joy of fulfilling our being by imposing upon us something we feel as hostile. It kills the freedom of answering creatively to what we encounter in things and men by making us look at a table of laws. It kills the ability to listen to the calling of the moment, to the voiceless voice of the others, and to the here and now. It kills the courage to act by the scruples of an anxiety-driven conscience. And in those who take it most seriously, it kills faith and hope and throws them into self-condemnation and despair.

There is no way out under the written code. The Spirit itself prevents us from becoming compromisers, half fulfilling, half defying the Commandments. The Spirit itself calls us back if we want to escape into indifference or lawlessness or the most usual escape: average self-righteousness. But when the Spirit calls us back from all this, it does so not in order to *keep* us under the written code, but in order to give us life.

How can we describe the life which the Spirit gives us? I could use many words, well known to everybody, spoken by Paul himself and after him by the great preachers and teachers of the church. I could say that the work of the Spirit, liberating us from the law, is freedom. Or I could say that its work is faith, or that its work is hope; and above all, I could say that the Spirit creates love, the love in which all laws are confirmed and fulfilled and at the same time overcome. But if I used such words, the shadow of the absent God would appear and make you and me aware that we cannot speak like this today. If we did, freedom would be distorted into willfulness, faith would be distorted into belief in the absurd, hope would be distorted into unreal expectations, and love—the word I would like most to use for the creation of the Spirit—would be distorted into sentimental feelings. The Spirit must give us new words or revitalize the old words to express true life. We must wait for them, we must pray for them, we cannot force them. But we know, in some moments of our lives, what life is. We know that it is great and holy, deep and abundant, ecstatic and sober, limited and distorted by time, fulfilled by eternity. And if the words are failing us in the absence of God, we may look without words at the image of Him in whom the Spirit and the Life were manifest without limits. AMEN.